Stephen Mason Merrill

The Crisis of this World

The Dominion and Doom of the Devil

Stephen Mason Merrill

The Crisis of this World
The Dominion and Doom of the Devil

ISBN/EAN: 9783337379636

Printed in Europe, USA, Canada, Australia, Japan

Cover: Foto ©Lupo / pixelio.de

More available books at **www.hansebooks.com**

THE CRISIS OF THIS WORLD

OR

THE DOMINION AND DOOM OF THE DEVIL

BY

S. M. MERRILL
BISHOP OF THE METHODIST EPISCOPAL CHURCH

———•—•———

CINCINNATI: CRANSTON & CURTS
NEW YORK: HUNT & EATON
1896

PREFACE.

THIS booklet is a sermon enlarged. Its theme has no great attraction for the average reader, but is of the highest importance to all lovers of truth. That the devil exists is a fact of tremendous significance. It has to do with almost every phase of Christian doctrine, and enters largely into the views one entertains of Christian experience, ethics, and work.

It will inevitably occur to the reader that this doctrine of angels perverted into devils, pervades the Scriptures too extensively, and in too great a variety of ways, to have no substantial basis in fact. It is impossible to construe the Scriptural language on this subject as figurative representations of myths or abstract principles. The Bible recognition of bad angels is as clear, as positive, as circumstantial, and as unmistakable as is its recognition of good angels. Whatever construction will exclude one class from actual existence will exclude the other class also. In our Savior's time the Sadducees denied the existence of angels and spirits, but the Pharisees confessed both. Our Lord and his apostles took the side of the Pharisees in this controversy. If they did not teach the existence of angels, good and bad, their words were wild and misleading, deceiving their own generation, and all the generations following.

The question of demonology naturally arises in connection with that of diabolism, but the limits here imposed do not admit of its elaboration. Whether demons, as recognized in the New Testament, were the departed souls of mortals who died in sin, or were a different order of existences, is a question not easily solved; but no such difficult question arises with regard to the devils which fell from angelic ranks. Whatever the nature or origin of demons, they are the subjects of the devil's kingdom, and under his sway. Their affiliation with fallen angels is complete, and their work and destiny the same.

Unless there is both diabolism and demonism in the Scriptures, the book is sealed to the understandings of men; its narratives are fables, its parables are riddles, and its revelations are as ambiguous as the oracles of pagan shrines. If there are no devils, the Bible doctrine of sin becomes more mysterious than ever, and the manifestation of the Son of God to take away sin and "destroy the works of the devil," assumes the character of a spectacular farce. Indeed, one hesitates to write the results of such dealing with the Scriptures as is necessary to eliminate this doctrine.

Recognizing the trend of popular thought to be in the direction of disregarding the seriousness of this feature of Divine revelation, and believing that the lightness with which it is ordinarily treated is subversive of vital piety, the conviction intensifies with meditation that some one ought to arrest the attention of the Church to the contents of the Bible on this subject, and point out the shallowness of the assumptions of so-called "liberalism" which pass so currently in these days as evidences of advanced thought. Wisdom demands sobriety in the study of such a theme, especially since superficiality has become emboldened to assert itself with such unblushing audacity. The truth is neither narrow nor illiberal, nor is it likely to suffer permanently from the application of opprobrious epithets. There is no philosophy against it; but there is need that attention be drawn to first principles and to the foundations. This little book is an effort to do this. Let it be read with the candor becoming the issue, and whether the reader's prepossessions accord with the current of its thought or not, let not its conclusions be thrust aside as antiquated and over-literal, till its positions are overthrown by the clearest possible expositions of the Sacred Word. With a sincere desire to encourage the study of the Holy Scriptures, and to secure reverent attention to the voice of God with regard to the profoundest mysteries of his universe, this little volume is sent forth to find its mission.

CONTENTS.

I.
THE CRISIS OF THIS WORLD, ... 11   PAGE.

II.
THE UNPARDONABLE SIN, ... 121

III.
THE DURATION OF PUNISHMENT, ... 155

I.

THE CRISIS OF THIS WORLD.

"Now is the judgment of this world: now shall the prince of this world be cast out."—JOHN XII, 31.

SOME Scriptures carry their meaning on their face, so that they can scarcely be misunderstood. Happily this is true of all that relate to morals and correctness of life; but in some instances where doctrines are concerned, and especially where the deep things of God which relate to his purposes and plans with reference to his triumph over the evil forces of the universe are involved, some study and careful meditation are necessary in order to apprehend the meaning of the expressions given. In the passage just read there is obscurity, which can only be removed by careful analysis. It contains two distinct propositions, each one seeming to be complete in itself, while a little study reveals mutual dependence, and shows particularly that the latter is explanatory of the former. It is therefore necessary that the two statements be considered together, and, if possible, so as to bring out the meaning of the entire passage.

Sometimes it is well in exposition to recall, or in some way recognize, the different views which have been taken of the Scripture in hand, before indicating the final interpretation to be insisted upon as correct. This is a preparatory exercise of the mind, and serves to remove difficulties, and to awaken anxiety to get at the truth, and to welcome it as a relief to the perplexities which arise in considering conflicting statements.

VARIOUS INTERPRETATIONS.

Among the various interpretations of this Scripture, which have received more or less favor, two or three are worthy of mention, and indeed must be considered, in order to do justice to the claims set forth in their behalf. Unfortunately for the interests of sound exegesis, it too often happens that hypotheses are framed for the purpose of pressing the obscure passage into the service of some particular doctrine, rather than with an unbiased aim to elicit exact truth. Scarcely any portion of the Sacred Word has escaped this ordeal, while this particular passage has stood in the presence of conflicting creeds like some rocky fastness, or vantage-ground in a great battle. The advocates of opposing doctrines have contended vigorously for its possession and support. As one looks upon the contentions of the past which have raged around it, the fact becomes apparent that it has been called to do service for doctrines which are foreign to its design and spirit, and to which it can only be made to yield a seeming support, under the manipulations of a criticism which is either superficial or violent.

It is evident that, whatever doctrine may gain support or suffer loss by the interpretation adopted, the sense of this passage must be determined by the application of the word "judgment." This is its ruling term, and its meaning must be ascertained before progress can be made in the study of the propositions it lays down. It involves the doctrine of the judgment to come in some way, although that doctrine is not its prominent thought.

There is an interpretation, which has received favor from eminent authorities, which carries with it no particular heresy, and from which no serious results would follow if it were accepted; but which, while plausible, can not be supported by the whole passage, nor by the application of other Scriptures containing similar terms. It holds that the words, "Now is the judgment of this world," relate to a fact then about to be accomplished, and which in a short time was actually consummated. The assumed fact is, that this world, through its courts and with legal formality, was about to judge and condemn its lawful Prince and Ruler in the person of Jesus Christ himself, and cast him out as a pretender, and as one unfit to live. That the powers of this world were about to do this thing is indisputable; for both the Jewish and the Roman authorities were ready to proceed against him, and to pronounce the judgment of condemnation which would result in his death. It was the hour and power of darkness that now prevailed. Why, then, is not this interpretation the true one, since its adoption involves no false doctrine, nor any serious practical difficulty?

It lacks exegetical soundness. In one respect it contravenes the truth. It implies, or rather assumes, that the phrase, "The prince of this world," points to him who uttered the words as the "prince" intended. In a highly important sense, Jesus Christ was the "Prince," the rightful Ruler, of this world, and of other worlds; but he never used this language with reference to himself. Wherever this phrase occurs, it designates another personage, an actual ruler in his sphere, but not a rightful ruler, whose expulsion from his dominion would be a wrong, or a disaster to any interest of humanity.

In another place the Savior uses these words: "Of judgment, because the prince of this world is judged." In this place the reference is to the work of the Spirit in reproving or convincing the world, and indicates the success of the work of the Spirit because of the successful judgment of "the prince of this world." In still another place he said: "Hereafter I will not talk much with you: for the prince of this world cometh, and hath nothing in me." In this place, when Christ referred to himself, he did not hesitate to use the personal pronouns "I" and "me;" and it is next to impossible to suppose that he would thus speak of himself, and then confuse his hearers by saying of himself, "The prince of this world cometh, and hath nothing in me," when he meant that he himself was that "prince," and therefore had all there was in him. He could not, and did not, mean that he himself was the "prince of this world." His thought was upon some one different from himself, and so different, and so completely separate in person and interest, that he could have nothing in common with himself; some one who was not interested in his mission or work, but was antagonized by it, and condemned through the ministry of the truth and the work of the Spirit, and could have neither lot nor part in his redemption: "He hath nothing in me." Therefore, any exposition that identifies "the prince of this world" with Jesus Christ is to be rejected.

Another interpretation requires quite as serious consideration, and perhaps more so, for the reason that it involves a very important doctrinal question. It is held as valid only by those who deny the future judgment, and assert a doctrine of judgment which places the retribution for sin, and all personal accountability, on this side of the grave, or at least this side of the resurrection of the dead. It is an insidious doctrine, easily clothed in Scriptural language, and liable to find acceptance where its relations and implications are not suspected. It does not deny or antagonize the judgment, nor the day of judgment, but explains it so as to break its force and destroy its moral power. It assumes that the day of judgment is now here; that the work of judgment is now going on; that men are now appearing before the judgment-seat of Christ, giving account of themselves, and receiving according to their deeds, and are therefore now in a state of actual retribution. In other words, it holds that "the day of judgment" is the gospel day; that the judgment is progressive, proceeding in parallel lines with God's kingly rule or divine government over men; and that it is particularly manifested under the gospel economy, relating largely, if not wholly, to the Divine dealings with men in a judicial way during life in this world. Its great point is the denial of any special period of judgment at the end of the gospel age, when rewards and punishments will be distributed for eternity. It thus alleges a present and progressive judgment, in opposition to the doctrine of a future general judgment at the last day, in connection with the resurrection of the dead; and in support of this notion, the first part of this Scripture is applied with great emphasis: "Now is the judgment of this world." It may be said without exaggeration that this text is the corner-stone of this edifice, the chief support of this whole doctrine of present retribution, which opposes and challenges belief in a final judgment-day at the end of the world. Remove this, and the superstructure falls. Can it be removed by fair interpretation?

A discussion of the doctrine of judgment, present or future, is not intended here; but the remark must be made that if this interpretation yields a doctrine clearly antagonized by the plainer teachings of our Lord, it can not be the right interpretation, and its alleged judgment is not the judgment alleged in this Scripture. Without looking further, it is enough to know that our Savior teaches another doctrine of judgment in this immediate connection, so that we need not look beyond this chapter to find the future judgment affirmed. He says: "I am come a light into the world, that whosoever believeth in me should not abide in darkness. And if any man hear my words, and believe not, I judge him not: for I came not to judge the world, but to save the world. He that rejecteth me, and receiveth not my words, hath one that judgeth him: the word that I have spoken, the same shall judge him at the last day." This explicit recognition of the time of the judgment "at the last day" is a complete refutation of the hypothesis which denies it, and is in full accord with all the direct teachings of the Scriptures on that subject. It contradicts the interpretation of the words before us, which assumes a present judgment, and forces us to seek a different meaning.

TRUE INTERPRETATION.

What, then, is the meaning of this Scripture? It has been looked upon as rather obscure, and yet it must have a meaning, and mean something valuable, if its real import can be caught; for our

Lord never used idle or meaningless words. As before said, its right interpretation must be determined by the word "judgment," and its application. There was a "judgment" which was near at hand; a judgment "of this world;" and a judgment which had intimate relation to the overthrow of "the prince of this world." It is a special judgment of world-wide results, looking to the conquest of whatever antagonizes the dominion of the Son of man.

The word "judgment" always means decision; and this is as true in the Greek as in the English. There is no judgment where there is no decision. In any court of justice, civil or criminal, a judgment rendered is a decision declared. If the word be used, as it often is, with reference to an exercise of the intellect, a mere mental process, a judgment formed is simply a decision arrived at in the mind, with regard to some question or problem pending. In fact, one can not conceive of the proper use of the word judgment where there is not a decision made or to be made. In the great day, when the question of human destiny shall be decided for weal or woe to every accountable being, that will be the final "judgment." In harmony with this thought, the day of judgment is called the day of decision—"the great decisive day."

Now, in the process of forming a judgment, whether it be a mere intellection, or the determination of the mind to a conclusion, or a decision formulated for expression or for legal declaration, there is a point where the mind turns towards a conclusion; where it sways from equipoise to the side of the prevailing reason or choice; where the preponderance of motive or argument becomes effective; and that point is the turning-point in the case and decision. It carries with it the whole power of the mind, and determines the outcome of the intellectual effort in weighing the merits of the case. It is the act formative of the judgment. The mind then turns to its conclusion, and rests in its judgment.

There are many turning-points in life. Each one is a decision. It determines something for us. These turning-points meet us at almost every step; they come unsought and unbidden, and they confront us with imperative demands. We must face them and accept the issue, whether we will or not. Some of them are more serious than others, because they touch more delicate phases of life, and carry into the future more that is vital to our well-being; but we are unable to see them or estimate their importance. In not a few instances the turning-point comes and goes without attracting the slightest attention at the time, and yet it is decisive of one's whole future. Perhaps it is a very little thing in itself, a mere incident, but its results will be felt through all the paths of life. It may be an ordinary business transaction, an introduction to a stranger, a passing social event, something that comes and goes as a matter of course, producing a momentary entertainment of pleasure or pain; or it may be an accident, a seeming blunder, or something neither sought nor desired; and yet, in after life, in its combinations with other things, it may be seen to have affected one's whole life. It may have been the most potent factor in deciding his business, or his place of abode, or his family connections, or the success or failure of some enterprise that had to do with his entire career. It was a turning-point, a decisive event.

These turning-points occur, not only in individual life, but in the life of families, of societies, of Churches, and of nations. They come when least expected, and are passed and their work done without observation; yet their influence is none the less powerful because unknown. There is a word which expresses to us the exact idea of a turning-point, and we often use it without a thought of its full meaning. It is the word *crisis*. In political life its use is quite familiar. There is always a *crisis* at hand when an election is pending. The turning-point is the election itself. That is the decisive event. A crisis always points to a pivotal event in one's life or history, or in the history of the family, Church, or nation. In every great enterprise there is a turning-point or *crisis*, when success or failure will be determined. There is a crisis in every battle. In every political campaign there is a crisis, sometimes more than one. The politician has keen eyes to discern the approach of the crisis. He sees just before him the turning-point which is to decide the country's fate for weal or woe—a *crisis*.

This word *crisis* answers exactly to the word "judgment" in this Scripture. It is a turning-point, or a decisive event, that is expressed or meant by the word judgment. It is the word used by the Lord in this place, so that no violence would be done the passage by reading it, "Now is the *crisis* of this world; now shall the prince of this world be cast out." The Son of man saw a turning-point in this world's affairs just at hand; something was about to occur that would be decisive, that would touch the interests of humanity for the future, that would decide the fate of the dominion of "the prince of this world," not for time alone, but for eternity as well—a *crisis!*

What could it be? It is not enough to speak here of an ordinary crisis; of a political occurrence of such significance as to determine the dynasty or the ruling power of the earth; for while such an event would be a crisis in the civil affairs of the nations, it would not reach the profound significance of these pregnant words, "the crisis of this world." Conjecture here will not do. We must know the decisive event. Happily there is no need of conjecture. The connection gives us the unmistakable identification of the event.

Jesus had just attended a feast in Bethany, where Mary anointed his feet and wiped them with the hairs of her head. Judas was there, and complained of the waste of expensive ointment. Then Jesus spoke of his burial. The next day was his triumphant entry into Jerusalem. It was the time of the Jewish passover, a great festival, with a great gathering of people. Among them were certain Greeks who came up to worship at the feast. They were anxious to see Jesus, whose fame had spread far and wide. They approached Philip, and said to him: "Sir, we would see Jesus." Philip told Andrew, and these two together told Jesus. In reply, Jesus made a brief address in their presence, and in the presence of the gathered assembly, which for comprehensiveness and profound thought was never excelled in human speech, not even in his own discourses. He said:

"The hour is come, that the Son of man should be glorified. Verily, verily,

I say unto you, Except a corn of wheat fall into the ground and die, it abideth alone; but if it die, it bringeth forth much fruit. He that loveth his life shall lose it; and he that hateth his life in this world shall keep it unto life eternal. If any man serve me, let him follow me; and where I am, there shall also my servant be: if any man serve me, him shall my Father honor. Now is my soul troubled; and what shall I say? Father, save me from this hour: but for this cause came I unto this hour. Father, glorify thy name."

As the people listened with awe and wonder, a strange sound was heard. It was not intelligible to the multitude, as the voice of God never is till the heart is opened by the Spirit of grace. "Then came there a voice from heaven, saying, I have both glorified it, and will glorify it again. The people therefore that stood by and heard, said that it thundered. Others said an angel spake to him. Jesus said, This voice came not because of me, but for your sakes. Now is the judgment of this world; now shall the prince of this world be cast out. And I, if I be lifted up from the earth, will draw all men unto me." The evangelist adds: "This he said, signifying what death he should die." There is no possibility of a mistake as to the event in his mind. The great event, which was the turning-point in human history and in the history of Divine government over men, was the death of Jesus Christ. For this purpose and for this hour he came. His birth and life were preparatory; his death was the climax. It was the culmination of his mission. In that event centered all human interest and human hope. It was the turning-point of destiny, the *crisis* of this world, the decisive hour for rulership in the spiritual realm.

This is the thought of this Scripture. How shall we estimate the magnitude of this *crisis?* From the beginning prophecy turned upon it. Inspired men, impelled by the Spirit of the Lord within them, wrote of it and wondered. Angels stooped from their high abode and bent their energies to grasp its meaning. They looked into it as we look into infinity. We see it as we see the ocean; as we see the immensity of space; as we see the stars in their eternal march. We get a glimpse of what transcends our powers, and humbly pause before the unmeasured depth of the fathomless abyss.

THE PRINCE.

The words that suggest the view now to be taken of this crisis are in this verse: "Now shall the prince of this world be cast out." This is an ultimate result. But who is "the prince of this world?" Why is he the prince of this world, and not of some other world? What the nature and boundary of his domain? Why cast him out? What is meant by casting him out? By what agency shall it be done? and what the result? Here is a field too large for full survey; but to some of these questions brief answers must be given.

With regard to the first question, some preparation for an answer has been made, but only negatively. It has been shown that "the prince of this world" was not the Christ himself. Jesus said of him very plainly: "He hath nothing in me." When Christ should be enthroned, this other prince should be cast out. They are antagonists. The only "prince" to be "cast out" by the death of Christ is the grand usurper of dominion in this world, God's chief adversary, the enemy whose works the Son of God came to destroy, the devil. He is a prince; the "prince of the devils;" the "prince of darkness;" "the prince of the power of the air, the spirit that worketh in the children of disobedience." He is "the god of this world, that hath blinded the minds of them that believe not." He is " the prince of this world."

We are thus brought face to face with the doctrine, not of devils, but the doctrine of the Holy Scriptures concerning the devils. What of all the doctrines has larger place in the discourses and parables of the Lord than this same doctrine concerning the devils? Nor is there any theme that mingles more freely with the writings of the apostles than the activity, vigilance, and ceaseless persistence of the devils, in corrupting human souls and seducing them from the truth. The miracle-working power of Christ was displayed in "casting out devils," perhaps more than in any other direction. Yet in our times, how seldom this subject enters the pulpit! How unwelcome the theme! One verily needs to apologize for preaching as did the Lord and his apostles.

Skepticism begins at this point. It becomes fashionable to speak lightly of devils and of Satanic influences. People doubt the existence of devils; treat them as myths and hobgoblins, and scowl them out of being, without serious thought. After a while they awake to the fact that the reasoning which discards devils, leads to the denial of angels and all spiritual existences, and finally to the denial of God. Most men deny the existence of the devil first, and then float on the waves of doubt till gross materialism sweeps them into the abyss of dismal agnosticism. When the devil and his kingdom are turned into a figure of speech, the descent into the darkness of atheism is easy.

From the pew also comes the exclamation, "What! does the minister believe in a personal devil? I thought the Church had discarded that belief." Perhaps some Churches have. Many Church members appear to have done so, and not a few preachers. Modern glossings of the Scriptures have mystified the people till the sophistries of unbelief have robbed them of the simplicity of faith. Imperfect conceptions of personality have done much to help on the progress of this subtle unbelief. It is so easy to confound personality with some form of bodily presence, and so hard to conceive of it as purely spiritual without body or parts. Verily there is need to look soberly at these things, as insidious poison so readily distills in the heart, and error abounds on every side, creeping into the Churches and pulpits of the land, with blinding and perverting power.

PERSONIFYING EVIL.

Let us look into this subject courageously. It is neither ethical nor scientific. Philosophy tells little about it. Yet the facts of human life are sunken into deeper mystery without than with the plain truths of revelation with regard to the existence of devils; and no truth in science or philosophy antagonizes our most literal interpretations of Scripture. A figure of speech! What a convenient thing it is to resolve every unpalatable truth into a rhetorical trope! With those who still respect the Scriptures, and yet deny the reality of devils, the popular assumption is that all Scriptural recognitions of the evil one are to be interpreted figuratively; that the principle of evil is personified and made the chief devil, "the prince of the devils;" and that the evil passions of men are metaphorically called devils. This might be labeled, "Important if true." It reduces the mission of the Son of God wonderfully. To destroy the works of such a devil was exceedingly expensive at the cost of such a price as the incarnation and death of Jesus Christ.

So great has been the influence of this notion of the personification of evil that it must be tested. It comes to us as a generalization, with little definiteness, and with sweeping pretentiousness, but unwilling and unable to endure subjection to analysis, or rigid application to particular Scriptures. It fails to meet the requirements of either the facts or the language of the Bible. These distinguish devils from men, and ascribe to them personal agency, qualities, powers, and activities, too distinctly and persistently to be transformed into personifications. Even figurative language is amenable to law. It is not necessarily vague because figurative. Any interpretation of it that will not stand appropriate tests must be condemned.

What is this principle of evil? Is it a chimera? Is it a nothing, or is it an entity? Where does it reside? What does it do? Is it not itself a devil? Is it any better than a devil? Is it less harmful, or its existence more easily accounted for? We must inquire into this thing, and pursue it as personificationists never think of doing. The concession that there is an evil principle is something. Whether it be physical or moral, it must have a nature and a residence, and some relation to human life and to the Divine government. If it exists and does the work of the devil, it should be so credited, and treated with the respect due to the devil.

Evil is a quality. It is the quality of something, and has no existence apart from its substance, whether its substance be matter, mind, or spirit. There is, then, no abstract principle of evil to be personified. The imagination is a powerful factor in human intellection; but the imagination, be it ever so brilliant, can not conceive of an abstract principle of evil actually existing outside of its substance, so as to admit of rational or logical personification. One can conceive of evil so as to abstract it in the mind; but to conceive of it as a principle existing in an abstract form, and working as an impersonal agent, is quite another thing, and impossible. There is, therefore, no abstract evil; no evil that does not exist as a quality inhering in some substance, agent, thing, or person. Keep this in mind. Evil is not a substance, but a quality; and it is a quality of something that has being; and that substance which has being is evil because of this quality which inheres within it. The substance or being takes its character from its qualities. This is true both in physics and in morals. Let us illustrate: Here is a piece of wood. You touch it and learn its qualities. At once you find two which are distinct, but never separated. They are hardness and smoothness. Both are real, and by mental effort you can abstract them, and think of each apart from the other; but they never so exist. The abstraction is purely mental. There is no hardness in the abstract, and no smoothness. There must be something that is hard, and something that is smooth, or these qualities can never exist. You can not imagine abstract life. It never so exists. There must be some living thing, or life has no place, no being. So it is with all spiritual things and qualities. There are moral qualities. These are predicated of spiritual entities. It is difficult to conceive of them otherwise than as so related. Certainly they never exist in the abstract, or apart from the substance or entity to which they belong. They inhere in something, and give character to something that is capable of moral character. There is no moral evil where there is no moral being capable of moral qualities. Moral qualities or principles do not float in the air, or reside in the sunshine or in the storm; they do not cleave to beasts or birds; they do not spring from the grass or the flowers. It is only in moral beings that moral qualities are found. They are found in men, because men are capable of moral action, and of moral character; and they are attributed to angels for the same reason. Goodness is a moral quality; but there is no moral goodness outside of some moral being that is good. It may be in men or angels, for these are capable of moral character, and may be good. Badness is a moral quality; but badness does not exist outside of its substance; and moral badness has no existence outside of moral beings that are bad. These may be men or angels, for both men and angels are capable of moral character. All the moral evil in the universe resides in moral beings. Let this be understood, and the question of the existence of devils is simplified. It is narrowed down to the question of the existence of moral evil outside of human beings. If it exists outside of human beings, it must be inside of some other beings; and these other beings, having intrinsic natures of the angelic grade, and being perverted by the qualities of evil they possess, are essentially corrupted angels, and therefore devils. Let the thought be reiterated: There is no moral evil where there is no moral nature. Men have moral natures, and moral evil dwells in men; and if there are no other beings possessing moral natures, then moral evil can not exist outside of men. It can not assail men from without; it can not lie in their pathway to entrap them; it can not approach them with evil solicitations; it can not seduce them into evil ways. Evil extrinsic to man in that event is powerless, for it has no being; and to all temptation from without, man's nature is impervious.

The Scriptures abound with warnings to men against the forces of moral evil that assail them from without, seeking to seduce and overcome them. Are these warnings from God? Is there truth in them? If not, then they are deceptive and misleading. They are doing the work of the devil; for he is a deceiver. This is his prime characteristic. But what deception can a non-entity impose? How can an abstraction mislead? In what way can a personification seduce? Who stands in awe of a metaphor? Either there are evil beings haunting the footsteps of men, pursuing them, tempting them, and sometimes leading them captive at will, or else needless warnings follow them, arousing needless fears of non-existent evils and impossible dangers.

The Scriptures teach two things concerning devils: First, that they exist;

and, second, that they tempt men and seek their ruin. Just here, as we enter the study of the Sacred Writings, with the view to find out their revelations concerning the devils, we are met with wonderings as to why fuller information has not been vouchsafed on a subject of such stupendous import. The same wonderment might arise with reference to many other things; but it is not for us to know the reasons for the limitations of knowledge within which we are confined. Our business is to keep within our limitations, and make the best of what we possess. The purpose of Divine inspiration is to reveal God, not the devils; and the disclosures made to us of these invisible powers are incidental, and only incidental, to the main purpose of the Bible. It is not strange, therefore, that our information is incomplete. Whatever is told us of the angels that sinned is for our warning, and not for the gratification of our curiosity. Of course, we often wish we could know more of the dark and mysterious things of the invisible world. It would gratify us to have the veil drawn aside, if but for a moment, or, with the young man with the prophet at Dothan, to have our eyes opened for a single gaze into the realm of the spiritual; but we must wait. Only slight glimpses are ours; and yet what wonderful things flash forth from out of the thick darkness, as lightnings in the storm, when God speaks of things unseen! The rift in the cloud shows measureless worlds beyond us.

SOME ERRORS.

Let us first correct some prevalent errors. These come largely from poetry. As Homer sang of the gods, so Milton and Dante and Pollok, and others, have sung of angels and devils. Poetic genius revels in the mysterious, and luxuriant fancy paints heroes and warriors, and victors and vanquished, with limitless rounds of conflict and peril and triumph, till thrones and dominions and powers move onward to final destiny at will. The pictures are brilliant, and affect the imagination; but they are only pictures. We must come down to facts. These are not numerous, but they are telling.

The first erroneous impression to be corrected has reference to the original abode of the angels that sinned. In popular thought these angels were once inhabitants of the heaven to which we aspire—the home of the good. A very thoughtful man of the legal profession once came to me with this line of thought: "If sin once entered heaven, why may it not enter there again? If angels in heaven once committed sin and were cast out, why may not others, and why may not the saints from earth rebel and fall? Why do you describe heaven as a holy place, and all its inhabitants as unalterably established in holiness, if some rebelled and lost its blessedness?" This man did not wish to be skeptical, but the popular view had brought serious difficulties into his mind. The looser faith, or non-faith, of Liberalism brought no relief, unless at the cost of some vital truth or Scriptural principle touching the divinity of Christ and atonement for sin, besides failing to explain the trend of the Scriptures with regard to the immanence of angels and spirits. Suggestions were made that relieved him, opening to the eye of faith a new vista, as he looked again into the broader sphere of the invisible. How marvelously the Bible enlarges vision and thought as we approach accuracy of interpretation!

Probation is the key to the profoundest mysteries. Now and then, persons are troubled with the thought that men on earth should be on trial, with destiny-making power in their hands, while superior intelligences were created in heaven, with none of the perils of probation to pass. Why should frail mortals be the exception? Is not the risk too great? Is not the responsibility disproportioned to our powers? Why should eternal consequences result from human action? Where else do we find such infinite effects from finite causes?

Some of these are hard questions. God has not yet given account of himself for some of his proceedings. We can not penetrate the motives of his rule, nor comprehend the reasons of all his appointments. General principles must guide where the fiery pillar of Revelation withholds its light from the pathway of our feet as we walk in this wilderness. Let us look steadily, and the stars in the firmament of Revelation will send glimmerings athwart the darkness, perhaps enough to lead us safely till the day dawns.

It appears to be not the exception, but the order of the universe, that rational, accountable beings, of all ranks and grades, should have a probational existence before confirmation in holiness. Were not "the angels that sinned" on probation? How else could they fall? What means the assertion that they "kept not their first estate?" It must be that, somewhere, they had an "estate" to keep, a law of life to obey, with confirmation in holiness conditioned on fidelity. What else can the Scriptures mean? It matters not that we have not been told where it was, nor what it was, nor how long they stood, nor why they fell; the essential thing is, that in "their first estate," within the "bounds of their own habitation," they were on trial, with a conditional blessedness before them, able to stand and free to fall. Their first estate was a probation. We know not its terms or tests, nor can we know its locality in the vast universe. Somewhere, within the dominion of the Almighty, they had their being, and their calling and privileges, and their duties and responsibilities; and, since inflexible justice is the rule of God's government, we must believe that their trial was a fair one. In their condition a fall was possible, but only possible by a willful abuse of power.

Let this thought be followed. If "the angels that sinned" were on probation, so also were those that did not sin.

May we not conclude that all angels were on trial in their "first estate?" If not, why not? Must it be assumed that all fell who were on probation, or who could fall? To our thought, human probation is not an exception, but the rule in the moral universe, a dim shadowing of angelic probation, the only condition suited to the free development of moral character under the universal government by rewards and punishments. Let it be understood, then, that somewhere in the domain of the King Eternal, and at some period in the limitless past, the angels of God were on probation; that, whatever the terms, some stood the test imposed, and were confirmed in holiness, and were exalted to the heaven of heavens, where apostasy is forever impossible; and that some failed to stand, and "left their own habitation," fell into open rebellion, and were cast down into *Tartarus*, the prison of darkness, to await the final judgment. These are the fallen angels, the devils. Their chief is Beelzebub, "the prince of the devils," "the prince of darkness," "the prince of this world."

The Scriptures speak of "war in heaven," when Satan and his hosts were cast out. That word "heaven" is a great word. In its wider use it means all the vast universe where sin does not abide. In the symbolical book of Revelation the apostasy of angels is described as war in heaven; but this does not antagonize the conception here given. In the end it will confirm it. But for the present it is enough to aver that there is no Scripture that teaches the popular thought which locates the sin of angels in the heaven of unchangeable blessedness.

The next error to be corrected is the

common assumption that the devils are already in their final abode, in the doom symbolized by the "lake of fire." This popular assumption does not accord with the Scriptures. On this point the testimony is more explicit than on the other. They are in *Tartarus*, the prison-house of darkness; but they are not in *Gehenna*. We speak of them as the inhabitants of hell, without defining the thought expressed or studying the exact meaning of the words. As yet they are this side the final judgment, this side of *Gehenna*, this side the "lake of fire," this side of their final doom. They are under "chains of darkness," but they are not physically bound. They are in the state which to us is invisible; but they have access to earth, and mingle with the affairs of mortals, in some way affecting our probation, disturbing our peace, and seeking our ruin. They incite men to evil ways, stir up their baser passions, instigate cruelty and crime, blind the understanding, deceive the thoughtless, and take captive the unwary. This they do during our probation; but when the judgment sits, and their final sentence falls upon them, they will pass into *Gehenna*, the final perdition, and then their career of temptation and war against the Church ends forever.

According to the testimony of Peter, "God spared not the angels that sinned, but cast them down to *Tartarus*, and delivered them into chains of darkness, to be reserved unto judgment." They are cast into prison, and held in custody, awaiting the judgment that will consign them to their endless doom. The language of Jude is much like this, but slightly more specific. It is: "And the angels which kept not their first estate, but left their own habitation, he hath reserved in everlasting chains under darkness unto the judgment of the great day." This word "reserved," in both these passages, has a meaning. It is used of the ungodly of the human race who have died, and are awaiting the judgment: "The Lord knoweth how to deliver the godly out of temptations, and to reserve the unjust unto the day of judgment to be punished." To "reserve" is to hold fast, to keep in custody. Prisoners under arrest, placed in prison for safe-keeping till court shall sit, are kept in custody, "reserved" unto the judgment of the court. So the angels that sinned are in prison, "reserved unto the judgment of the great day," not to be released, but "to be punished"—punished by being cast into "everlasting fire, prepared for the devil and his angels." In the Apocalyptic vision of "the judgment of the great day," after Satan had been in the "bottomless pit," and after he had been "loosed for a little season," deceiving the nations which are in the four quarters of the earth, it is written: "And the devil that deceived them was cast into the lake of fire and brimstone, where the beast and false prophet are, and shall be tormented day and night for ever and ever." This final doom comes after "the judgment of the great day," and after the whole period of temptation and warfare against the Church, and after the imprisonment in *Tartarus* under chains of darkness. It is therefore after the close of the reign of sin on the earth, and after the end of the gospel dispensation. "And death and hell were cast into the lake of fire. This is the second death."

From all this it appears unmistakable that the devil and his angels have not yet reached their final doom. They are beyond their time of probation, imprisoned in the world of darkness, awaiting the coming of the great day, when their final punishment is sure. In the meantime their imprisonment does not destroy their activity. Their chains of darkness do not impede their locomotion within their limits. Having passed their own probation, and fallen, they become an element in ours. They find access to mortals on this mundane sphere, and here on earth they war against the Lord and against his Anointed. Here is the citadel of their power, and here, as nowhere else in the universe, their flag of rebellion waves defiance to the army of God. The "prince of darkness" is now "the prince of this world." He is "the prince of the power of the air."

IMMANENCE OF THE INVISIBLE.

There are some things here which are "hard to be understood." The fact that the fallen angels are imprisoned "under chains of darkness," dwelling in *Tartarus*, and are yet in this world tempting and seeking to govern the children of men, is a mystery. We own it such, and yet we know that much of the mystery grows out of our habits of thought, and our unarranged impressions with regard to the invisible world. It is so hard for us to conquer the feeling that the world of darkness is necessarily very far off. Although invisible, it is not far away physically. It is a spiritual world, and very near to us. Its lines touch the world we live in, and its borders overlap the scenes of our daily lives, pressing hard upon our pathway when we least suspect the presence of the unseen. If our eyes could be opened, we might behold troops of angels, good and bad, covering the mountains and valleys about us, as the horsemen and chariots of God surrounded Elisha on the mountain at Dothan, when the Lord opened the young man's eyes in the presence of the prophet. There are more things in heaven and earth than human philosophy has ever dreamed of. As the earth floats enwrapped in its own atmosphere, so is it surrounded by the unseen forces of the spiritual world. The relation of the visible and the invisible is more intimate than our material senses can discern or verify. We can not apprehend the spiritual phenomena with which Revelation is burdened till we catch the thought that only the veil of flesh and blood shuts us in from the world of spiritual realities— a world too subtle for our dull senses to detect, and too vast for our present powers to comprehend.

This immanence of the invisible explains much, while it expands our thoughts, giving us a wider horizon than is otherwise possible; but still our vision is circumscribed, and we are unable to pass the limitations of our being. We stand in awe in the presence of the deeper mysteries which encompass us, knowing that just beyond lies the realm of the unsearchable. We should not, therefore, stagger at the thought confronting us, that the angels which "left their own habitation," wherever that was, and lost the hope of the higher heaven, found their way to this newly-endowed earth, and here planted the throne of the kingdom of darkness. Here, under the leadership of "the prince of darkness," they found the human pair in the garden of innocence, laid siege to their hearts through their senses, and seduced them from their allegiance to God. Thus, gaining ascendency in human hearts, they began the contest for the dominion of this world. Here Satan established his seat. Here gathered all the forces of evil. Here assembled "the rulers of the darkness of this world," "the wicked spirits on high!" In the light of this truth the reason dawns upon us why it is that "the prince of the devils," "the prince of darkness," is also "the prince of this world," and must be cast out as the kingdom of God is established and grows upon the earth.

In further considering this thought, the Scriptures alone can guide us to an adequate recognition of the presence and dominion of the devils in this world, and their connection with the affairs of men. The question is one of fact, and since the fact depends not on any philosophy we can comprehend, progress can not be made in its study except in following the light of the Sacred Word, accepting its testimony, and walking steadily whithersoever it leads. In its relation to goodness, sin is discordant and destructive; but within its domain it appears to be a bond of union. Its virus penetrates the natures of all classes whom it touches. Men and devils are made akin through its blight. "Whosoever committeth sin is of the devil." It is therefore more than a figure of speech when wicked men are called "the children of the devil." As sin is of the devil, wherever sin reigns, there is the kingdom of the wicked one, and there his dominion.

SATAN AND JOB.

The thought that Satan has much to do with men in this world pervades the

Scriptures. It is possible that the book of Job is the oldest book in the world. Whatever of revision or adaptation of its language may have occurred at a later date, its conception of God and of the social and religious life of the people antedates Moses. Its life is pre-eminently patriarchal and pastoral, and its pictures of worship such as prevailed before idolatrous corruptions were widely diffused. Whatever view one takes of the imagery of this book, it must be understood that its representation of Satan's presence and power accords with the belief of the times, and stands forth approved of God. He appears here not as a myth, nor as a personification, but as a veritable agent, acting a part in keeping with the character he bears as the enemy of God and men. "When the sons of God came to present themselves before the Lord, Satan came also among them." If in this representation there is somewhat of dramatic dressing, it harmonizes well with Oriental thought, and expresses the real character and habit of Satan. Recognizing his presence, the Lord said unto him: "Whence comest thou?" The answer comes as from one conscious of the folly of evasion in the presence of his interrogator: "Then Satan answered the Lord and said, From going to and fro in the earth, and from walking up and down in it." The Lord makes no dissent, and no hint is found that this was a false answer; nor is there any suggestion in the answer, or out of it, that Satan's real dwelling-place was in some far-off world, or that his visits to this world were occasional, extraordinary, or by special permission. The fact that God gave him special permission to touch Job's prosperity is suggestive of limitations of his power with reference to those whom God protects. His agency in bringing the Sabeans and the Chaldeans, and the fire and the wind, and finally the sore boils, to complete the calamities which befell this holy man, furnishes a fruitful study with regard to his ability to instigate wicked men and to control the elements of physical nature; but our present concern is with his uncontradicted assertion that his dwelling-place is so intimately related to this world. While nothing can be affirmed on the naked word of "the father of lies," yet even his declaration, under circumstances where contradiction would be certain, if false, may shed light on questions relating to his pretensions and power. His is a life of ceaseless activity. He came "from going to and fro in the earth, and from walking up and down in it." It is not impossible that the apostle Peter had this statement in mind when he said: "Your adversary, the devil, as a roaring lion, walketh about, seeking whom he may devour." At the very least, this apostolic recognition of his whereabouts and of his habit, confirms the thought expressed that his sphere of activity is here amongst men.

CHRIST TEMPTED.

The record of our Lord's temptation, after his baptism, is pertinent to the subject in hand. How naturally the presence of the devil is recognized here, and throughout the Gospels! Not the least surprise is manifested that he should appear at any time or in any place. He comes and goes as if upon his native heath! After the baptism at the Jordan, "Jesus was led of the Spirit into the wilderness to be tempted of the devil." What was really done is mentioned in the Scriptures as done of design. The discipline of the Son of man was not complete till the devil had exhausted his power of temptation upon him. We are not to explain his methods. In some way he came to Jesus. Whether in bodily shape like a man, or whether in mental action alone, retaining invisibility, is indifferent to the present issue. He came in his own character as the tempter. Necessarily there is mystery in his movements. But he came to Jesus. The temptation was from without. It was not in any sense the action of the body, mind, temper, passions, or imagination of the Son of man himself. He was not his own tempter. There was nothing in his nature to fill such an office. The devil was not, therefore, an evil passion of human nature. Neither was he the personification of an abstract principle of evil. The evangelists who describe this temptation were not writing poetry. They recorded substantial facts for the common people, as well as for the learned, and the facts are incompatible with any hypothesis of temptation from an impersonal devil.

After forty days of fasting, the temptations began. Three distinct assaults are described. The first was an attempt to take advantage of a physical need, through a natural appetite, to induce an unwarranted exercise of miraculous power. "And when the tempter came to him, he said, If thou be the Son of God, command that these stones be made bread." This suggestion, under the circumstances, shows discrimination and sagacity. Jesus repelled it at once by the use of Scripture: "It is written, Man shall not live by bread alone, but by every word that proceedeth out of the mouth of God." Foiled in this attempt, the devil resorts to the weapon by which his first assault had been defeated. He quotes Scripture. "Then the devil taketh him up into the city, and setteth him on a pinnacle of the temple, and said unto him, If thou be the Son of God, cast thyself down, for it is written, He shall give his angels charge concerning thee, and in their hands they shall bear thee up, lest at any time thou dash thy foot against a stone." The promptness of the repulse appears in the brevity of the record: "Jesus said unto him, It is written again, Thou shalt not tempt the Lord thy God." From this reply it was evident to the tempter that this man would do nothing rash or presumptuous. His next effort was an appeal to what in most men of strength is their most vulnerable point, their love of power and dominion: "Then the devil taketh him up into an exceeding high mountain, and sheweth him all the kingdoms of the world, and the glory of them; and saith unto him, All these things will I give thee—for that is delivered unto me, and to whomsoever I will, I give it—if thou wilt fall down and worship me." Then, in reply to this open proposal, the climax of effrontery, came from Jesus the word of authority and power which ended the contest: "Get thee hence, Satan; for it is written, Thou shalt worship the Lord thy God, and him only shalt thou serve."

One of the troubles encountered in studying this mysterious conflict between Christ and Satan arises from an almost irrepressible desire to understand the mode of the processes declared. One naturally asks how the devil took the Savior of men into the mountain, and into the city, and how he set him on a pinnacle of the temple. But the how of these movements is not revealed. Whether they were merely transportations of the mind, or whether a physical movement of the body from place to place was meant, or whether supernatural power removed the persons to the points named, may be well left among the unexplained incidents of the transaction. The great facts of the temptation are given without any attempt to make known the mode of the facts. The audacious assault was made upon the integrity of the Son of man, and it was promptly and effectually repelled.

Sometimes the remark has been made that when Satan offered to give to Christ all the kingdoms of the world and the glory of them, he was indulging a bit of vain boasting, as he was promising what was not his own, and what he had no power to convey. This, however, is not so clear. He had by usurpation acquired control of "the vain pomp and glory of this world," and had so far subjected it to himself, that, in throwing off his yoke, and in avowing allegiance to Christ, in baptism, it is necessary to renounce the devil and all his works, the vain pomp and glory of this world, and the carnal desires of the flesh. These are all of his kingdom. Proof is not wanting that he holds dominion in the high places of the earth. In courts of royalty his power is next to supreme. If love of worldliness is opposition to God, then the devil exults in the palaces of kings. If tyranny is hateful to God, the places of worldly power are the delight of the enemy of righteousness. If the lust of lucre is inimical to holiness, Satan has his seat in municipal governments. Alas! it is too true that "the prince of the devils" is "the prince of this world." His throne and kingdom are here—here by usurpation, but here in fact as a reigning power.

THE DEVIL IN PARABLES.

The parables of our Lord can not be interpreted without the recognition of the presence and power of the devil in this world. Two in particular will illustrate this declaration. Read the parable of the Sower and the Seed, with the Lord's own exposition of it. Bear in mind, also, that the exposition is not parable, but plain, literal truth. It is too common, when one finds in the parables unwelcome doctrine, to say: "O, well, it is only a parable, and perhaps we do not get its meaning." Nothing of the kind can occur here; for the exposition of the parable removes all uncertainty as to its meaning: "The seed is the word of God. Those by the wayside are those that hear; then cometh the devil, and taketh away the word out of their hearts, lest they should believe and be saved." The activity and vigilance of the devil is the basal thought. Wherever the gospel of the kingdom is preached, there is the devil ready to intercept the truth, or to counteract it by diverting attention, or filling the mind with other things. Not that the devil is everywhere, as if omnipresent; but there are legions of them, all alert and intensely earnest in opposing the work of God. Read, also, the parable of the Tares of the Field. It is a parable, but it has a meaning: "The kingdom of heaven is likened unto a man which sowed good seed in his field; but while men slept, his enemy came and sowed tares among the wheat, and went his way. But when the blade was sprung up, and brought forth fruit, then appeared the tares also. So the servants of the householder came and said unto him, Sir, didst not thou sow good seed in thy field? From whence then hath it tares? He said unto them, An enemy hath done this. The servants said unto him, Wilt thou then that we go and gather them up? But he said, Nay; lest while ye gather up the tares ye root up also the wheat with them. Let both grow together until the harvest: and in the time of harvest I will say to the reapers, Gather ye together first the tares, and bind them in bundles to burn them; but gather the wheat into my barn." Now for the meaning of this parable. It is neither guess-work nor inference; nor is it conjecture. It is given by the Divine authority, with every element of uncertainty eliminated. The multitude who heard the parable had dispersed, and the disciples came to him in the house, and said to him, " Declare unto us the parable of the tares of the field." "He answered and said unto them, He that soweth the good seed is the Son of man; the field is the world; the good seed are the children of the kingdom; but the tares are the children of the wicked one; the enemy that sowed them is the devil; the harvest is the end of the world; and the reapers are the angels. As therefore the tares are gathered and burned in the fire: so shall it be in the end of this world. The Son of man shall send forth his angels, and they shall gather out of his kingdom all things that offend, and them which do iniquity; and shall cast them into a furnace of fire: there shall be wailing and gnashing of teeth. Then shall the righteous shine forth as the sun in the kingdom of their Father. Who hath ears to hear, let him hear."

When the Lord talked thus to his disciples, to whom was to be committed the task of unfolding the mysteries of his kingdom after his departure from earth, he threw off the covering and drapery of the parable, and spoke plainly, pointedly, and literally, of the agencies of evil to be encountered in the world, and of the outcome of the world-wide and age-lasting conflict. By no possible interpretation can his words be made to mean anything other than that "the field is the world." It is just as literally true that "the tares are the children of the wicked one." Nor can there be any propriety in trying to modify the words, "The enemy that sowed them is the devil." Satanic agency in the wickedness of human lives could not be more positively asserted in human speech.

DEVIL WORSHIP.

Another illustration of the dominion of the devil in this world, showing the height of his presumptuous claims as its ruling "prince," is found in the fact that, as the ambitious rival of the Deity, he delights in being worshiped, and appropriates to himself all the worship paid to idols and false divinities. This dominant ambition displayed itself when, at the climax of his supreme audacity, he proposed that the Son of man should fall down and worship him. He is the presiding divinity in every pagan temple on the earth, the god of every idolatrous altar and shrine. To him are offered the sacrifices and the incense of all the false worship of the ages. Not that he is always known, or that the honors paid to idols are consciously intended for him by the worshipers; that is not necessary to his purpose or scheme. He delights in the false; he revels in the deceptions and ignorance of his victims; he gloats over the impurities and degradation of men. His sphere is darkness and his reign is death. Why, then, should he seek to be known? That is not his aim. He is worshiped in ignorance, and delights in service not his own, except so far as whatever is false and impure is his.

In the book of Deuteronomy we read: "But Jeshurun waxed fat and kicked; thou art waxen fat, thou art grown thick, thou art covered with fatness; then he forsook God which made him, and lightly esteemed the Rock of his salvation. They provoked him to jealousy with strange gods, with abominations provoked they him to anger. They sacrificed unto devils, not to God; to gods whom they knew not, to new gods that came newly up, whom your fathers feared not." (Deut. xxxii, 15–17.) "And they shall no more offer their sacrifices unto devils, after whom they have gone a whoring. This shall be a statute forever unto them throughout their generations." (Leviticus xvii, 7.) When the psalmist summed up the faults of the people of Israel in their apostasies, he said: "They were mingled with the heathen, and learned their works. And they served idols which were a snare unto them. Yea, they sacrificed their sons and their daughters unto devils, and shed innocent blood, even the blood of their sons and of their daughters, whom they saacrificed unto the idols of Canaan." (Psalm cvi, 35–38.) Among the heinous sins of Jeroboam and his sons, the fact is recorded that they "cast off the Levites from being priests unto the Lord, and he ordained him priests for the high places, and for the devils, and for the calves which he had made." (2 Chron. xi, 15.)

It will be claimed that these Old Testament records, which were intended to portray the baseness and degradation of the worshipers of idols, regard all idols as devils, because the divinities represented by the idols were rivals of the God of Israel, and were therefore adversaries, or devils, in the estimation of the loyal worshipers of the living God. This is certainly true, but it is not the whole truth. These idols were not called devils because they were dumb and senseless, nor because they drew away the people after them. The thought is not conveyed that devils are nothing more than these stupid blocks of wood and stone. The idol stood for a divinity that was not seen; for an invisible agency, with intelligence and power and activity; for an unseen force, which was gifted in bewitching and corrupting the people, doing for them and with them the things which the Scriptures uniformly ascribe to fallen angels or devils. It was therefore natural to speak of idols as devils, and of idol-worship as devil-worship. He who blinds and deceives men, and leads them into corrupted and corrupting worship, is the devil.

The Apostle Paul took a realistic view of this subject, and without hesitation or reservation pronounced all idol-worship devil-worship: "Behold Israel after the flesh: are not they which eat of the sacrifices partakers of the altar? What say I then? that the idol is anything, or that which is offered in sacrifice to idols is anything? But I say, that the things which the Gentiles sacrifice, they sacrifice to devils, and not to God: and I would not that ye should have fellowship with devils. Ye can not drink the cup of the Lord, and the cup of devils: ye can not be partakers of the Lord's table, and of the table of devils." (1 Cor. x, 18–21.) The apostle was neither dramatic nor rhetorical in this appeal; but earnest, terse, and nervous in his utterance, evidently feeling that the subject in hand required plainness and strength, rather than ornament. "Fellowship with devils" was not to be tolerated, and yet that dreadful thing stood before him as a menace to the work of God. It was a living danger, not to receive dallying, but denunciation; and yet in expressing the indignation within him, he must avoid conceding that the idol was anything in itself. Whatever the idol was, or whatever its name or form, or whatever it expressed in symbol to the worshiper, in the apostle's enlightened conception the devil was behind the idol, and claimed the honor and the adoration, and his was the fellowship. The altar and the sacrifice were his—his, in fact, because they were false and corrupting, and his because of his instigation. Thus it is with all idolatries, whether formal or informal, whether visible or invisible, whether material or spiritual, whether in heathen or in Christian lands. He whose worship is false, worships only the devil.

In the record of the disasters which follow the sounding of the sixth trumpet, in the Apocalyptic vision, it is written: "And the rest of the men which were not killed by these plagues yet repented not of the works of their hands, that they should not worship devils, and idols of gold, and silver, and brass, and stone, and of wood, which neither can see, nor hear, nor walk." (Rev. ix, 20.) With their gross conceptions of the character of their gods, and with their faint perception of moral distinctions, and their benumbed sensibilities, it is scarcely strange that worshipers of idols fail to distinguish between good and bad divinities, and think only of powers supposed to be able to harm them in anger, and able to favor them if propitiated by sacrifice. With them, divinities and devils are nearly related. Their gods at best are scarcely better than devils, and their worship is such as devils approve. The moral natures of men absorbed in the pursuit of gold, worshiping only at the shrine of mammon, become as morbid and sensual, as obtuse to spiritual things, and as thoroughly deadened to the claims of righteousness, as those who worship images made of gold, or silver, or stone, or wood. While they would scout the intimation as preposterous and offensive, they are in fact worshipers of idols and devils.

DELIVERED FROM SATAN.

Another fact which declares with marked emphasis the power of Satan over human souls is, that in the Scriptures the conversion of a sinner is regarded, in every instance, as a soul delivered from the dominion of the devil. This appears in the commission given the Apostle Paul at the time of his own conversion. His fullest statement of the scope of his commission is found in his address delivered in the presence of Agrippa, Acts xxvi, 15–18: "And I said, Who art thou, Lord? And he said, I am Jesus whom thou persecutest. But rise, and stand upon thy feet: for I have appeared unto thee for this purpose, to make thee a minister and a witness both of these things which thou hast seen, and of those things in which I will appear unto thee; delivering thee from the people, and from the Gentiles, unto whom now I send thee, to open their eyes, and to turn them from darkness to light, and from the power of Satan unto God, that they may receive forgiveness of sins, and inheritance among them which are sanctified by faith that is in me." No grander conception of the gospel ministry was ever expressed in human speech. Its aim is to "turn men from darkness to light, from the power of Satan unto God." Before the gospel reaches them, they are in "darkness," and under "the power of Satan." The gospel of God is light, a light shining in darkness, banishing ignorance, superstition, and unbelief. It is also the gospel of power. It breaks the bonds in which Satan holds his captives, and gives them freedom. It lifts them out of death into life. After exercising this commission till full proof was made of it, this apostle exultingly describes the result of his ministry: "Giving thanks unto the Father, which hath made us meet to be partakers of the inheritance of the saints in light; who hath delivered us from the power of darkness, and hath translated us into the kingdom of his dear Son: in whom we have redemption through his blood, even the forgiveness of sins." Here are the blessings he was commissioned to bear to the Gentiles. Under his preaching they were "turned from darkness to light, from the power of Satan unto God," and fitted for this higher fellowship and this nobler inheritance. From being slaves to the devil, they become the Lord's freemen.

A leading truth, firmly grasped, sheds light on incidental and subordinate matters which are enveloped in deep obscurity when standing alone. The doctrine that Satan rules in the kingdom of darkness, in which the ungodly abide, illustrates what is otherwise difficult of interpretation in the apostolic Church. Paul speaks of persons excommunicated or cut off from the fellowship of the Church for open wickedness, as "delivered unto Satan." After the failure to reform or correct their lives by proper instruction and discipline, they were pronounced incorrigible, and given up as hopeless. They were simply abandoned to their former state. The ecclesiastical withdrawal of the fellowship of the Church was the act of delivering the offender over to Satan. The expression is strong; for the act was one of deep solemnity, and meant much to those whose views of the powers of darkness accorded with the Scriptures.

The apostle's description of the qualification and work of a minister follows in this line, implying the same thing. Its incidental testimony is not less convincing because incidental: "And the servant of the Lord must not strive; but be gentle unto all men, apt to teach, patient; in meekness instructing those that oppose themselves; if God peradventure will give them repentance to the acknowledging of the truth; and that they may recover themselves out of the snare of the devil, who are taken captive by him at his will." (2 Tim. ii, 24–26.) All who resist the truth, "oppose themselves." They stand in their own light; they disregard their highest interests, while thinking to serve themselves; their spiritual vision is obstructed by overhanging clouds of worldliness. Moreover, they are in "the snare of the devil." These are strong words, much too strong to be meaningless. Behind them there is a condition, a moral estate, abnormal it may be, but a veritable condition of thralldom, in which the soul is held as a prisoner in the hands of an adversary. It is "taken captive by him at his will." Thus are all the unsaved. They are under the dominion of the devil, and can only "recover themselves" by "repentance to the acknowledging of the truth."

It is thought by some to be a sort of illiberal species of bigotry to assign all the unsaved to the kingdom of darkness, and to regard wicked men as being under the power of the devil. This may be done sometimes in the spirit of bigotry; but it is well to be sure who does it, and in what spirit, before permitting indignation to burn against it with consuming heat. To whose kingdom do the wicked belong? The beloved apostle, whose spirit was richly imbued with the love of the Master and with love to men, said: "In this the children of God are manifest, and the children of the devil: whosoever doeth not righteousness is not of God, neither he that loveth not his brother." Nor is this language any stronger than that used by the Savior himself. The Jews said to Jesus: "We have one Father, even God." This is the chief delusion of the unregenerate. They assume that they can be God's children without being born again. Jesus flatly denied their claim in this respect, and once for all condemned such pretensions. He said, in reply: "If God were your Father, ye would love me: for I proceeded forth and came from God; neither came I of myself, but he sent me. Why do ye not understand my speech? even because ye can not hear my word. Ye are of your father the devil, and the lusts of your father ye will do." (John viii, 41–44.) If it be true that "the tares are the children of the wicked one," and if, as the beloved disciple has said, "Whosoever committeth sin is of the devil," and if the prince of the devils rules in the empire of darkness, then to look upon the race of ungodly men as belonging to the kingdom of the devil, is not going beyond the clearest possible Scripture warrant; and any charge of narrowness or bigotry which this position involves, lies with full force against the Lord himself and his holy apostles.

The Jews to whom Christ talked so plainly were typical men in some respects. They were not atheists; neither were they profligates. After their fashion they were religious. They were lineal descendants of Abraham, and within the covenant in the literal sense; but spiritual blindness was upon them. Their claim was: "We have one Father, even God." It was no doubt very abrupt and extremely offensive when the Lord said to them: "Ye are of your father the devil." Their "liberalism" was shocked. He was too literal! Paul found one of this kind on the island of

Cyprus—one who opposed the apostle, and tried to turn the deputy, a convert, away from the faith. The Spirit of God came upon the apostle, and, moved by a sacred impulse, Paul "set his eyes on him," and pronounced such words as a desperate case demanded: "O, full of all subtilty and all mischief, thou child of the devil, thou enemy of all righteousness, wilt thou not cease to pervert the right ways of the Lord?" Such plainness of speech appears to many to be quite illiberal. No doubt Elymas thought Paul a bigot! But the blindness which fell on his natural vision was the fit symbol of the state of his mind with regard to the things of God.

Truth is not the less truth because unwelcome. Wicked men are none the less certainly the children of the devil because they do not like to believe it. False teachers can afford to be liberal.

They are always broad. Like the master they serve, they have no fondness for any "narrow way." As there were false prophets of old, so were there "false apostles" in the days of the apostles, "deceitful workers, transforming themselves into the apostles of Christ. And no marvel: for Satan himself is transformed into an angel of light. Therefore it is no great thing if his ministers be transformed as the ministers of righteousness; whose end shall be according to their works." (2 Cor. xi, 14, 15.) Ministers of Satan, transformed into ministers of righteousness, never claim for Satan what is his own. In this they are singular among men, but in harmony with their master. Satan does not wish to be known, and his agents never proclaim his presence or his power. He works in the darkness, and hates the light. His ministers please him by denying him, and denying his existence; therefore they are never heard warning men, as did the apostles of Christ, "lest they fall into the condemnation of the devil." Of all men they are the most "liberal," the most advanced in lines of worldly thought, the most prompt to disclaim against bondage to creeds, and the readiest to assure the devotees of pleasure and sin that there is neither devil nor danger. God's prophet Ezekiel had to do with such teachers in his day, and his burning words of denunciation apply with undiminished force to all who deal with God's Word deceitfully: "Because with lies ye have made the righteous sad, whom I have not made sad; and strengthened the hands of the wicked, that he should not return from his wicked way, by promising him life!"

THE DEVIL WARS WITH BELIEVERS.

The next fact to be noticed has special significance in this study. It is, that the devil pursues believers after they are converted, making the Christian life a continuous conflict with spiritual foes, as well as with the infirmities of the flesh and the allurements of the world.

The disciples of Christ were assailed by the devil from the beginning. To Simon Peter the Master said: "Satan hath desired to have you, that he might sift you as wheat; but I have prayed for thee, that thy faith fail not." It was a case of special peril, which the Savior foresaw, and in view of which he forewarned his servant, and forearmed him for the conflict, the memory of which warning must have flashed upon Peter's mind with peculiar power when the reproving look of Jesus arrested his attention after his wretched denial. The event illustrates the devil's vigilance and the Savior's solicitude. The same evil power was successful with one of the twelve. The apostasy of Judas and his betrayal of Christ must be ascribed to Satanic influence: "After the sop, Satan entered into him." The disciples at Rome were in sore trials when the Apostle Paul comforted them with the assurance that the "God of peace shall bruise Satan under your feet shortly." He also himself found it necessary to be on his guard against the machinations of the devil, as he expressed the danger: "Lest Satan should get an advantage of us; for we are not ignorant of his devices." On one occasion, when he had been unable to accomplish a cherished purpose, which was to visit Thessalonica, he attributed his failure to the fact that "Satan hindered us." This apostle's writings teem with recognitions of the industry and power of the great adversary, and of the necessity of watchfulness on the part of Christians in order to avoid his interruptions; and yet they abound with expressions of perfect confidence in the ability of Christ to keep his people in safety from all the blandishments and evil schemes of this malignant foe. His descriptions of the reigning power of the devil tend to enhance the value of the Christian's triumph by faith. He wavers not, nor would he have any one falter because of any power Satan possesses in this world. The burden of his thought accords with the words of the Apostle James: "Resist the devil, and he will flee from you."

The apostle gives us his fullest portrayal of the believer's conflicts with the powers of darkness, in his Epistle to the Ephesians. It is well to study the picture in its lights and shades, in its scope and in its terms. We shall find in it the ring of battle and the shout of victory: "Finally, my brethren, be strong in the Lord, and in the power of his might. Put on the whole armor of God, that ye may be able to stand against the wiles of the devil. For we wrestle not against flesh and blood, but against principalities, against powers, against the rulers of the darkness of this world, against spiritual wickedness in high places;" or, as in the margin, and more literal, "against wicked spirits on high." This whole conflict is with invisible forces, all external to the one who battles against them, capable of assault, of "wiles," schemes, and devices, for the purpose of carrying out a nefarious purpose. "That ye may stand against the wiles of the devil." As the chief adversary he plans the battle; he marshals the forces and forms the combinations. The rulers of the darkness of this world, the wicked spirits on high, forming principalities and powers, all move at his command.

This one phrase includes all the spiritual enemies of the believer, the other parts of the passage being explanatory or subordinate to this. "The wiles of the devil!" How suggestive these words! They indicate personality, shrewdness, skill, strategy, and power. This devil is, therefore, neither an abstraction nor a figure of speech. Nor yet is he a human passion. He is no part of "flesh and blood." The negative points in this description are full of meaning: "We wrestle not against flesh and blood." This is as definite as it is comprehensive. It is not a physical warfare. The words mean this and more. They mean that the opposition comes from outside of human nature. All the human agencies and forces of evil are included in the words "flesh and blood;" but here are enemies which are not "flesh and blood." They are not merely spiritual, but they are "spirits," "wicked spirits on high." They are in combination against good, under the leadership of the "prince of the devils." This invisible chieftain musters the wicked spirits of the universe, forms them into "principalities and powers," constitutes them "the rulers of the darkness of this world," and leads them forth to assail the Church of Christ, and to conquer individual believers. Wicked men, and sometimes civil and municipal governments, join in the fight against righteousness, becoming the unconscious instruments of unseen forces; but their agency is not that which the apostle here recognizes. All visible agencies, all purely human powers, all human passions, combinations, governments, machinations, and animosities, are embraced in the phrase "flesh and blood." The fight is not against these, except as these are instigated, directed, and used by the devil, whose "wiles" take in the employment of all instrumentalities available for his purposes. He employs instruments, and he reaches the soul through the senses of the body, and through the passions of the flesh, and through the infirmities of corrupted human nature; but it is a mistake to regard that which is an instrument as an agent, or the avenues of the devil's approach to the soul, as the devil himself.

In this warfare against the devil and his "wiles" and devices, we need the armor which the gospel provides. It is a defensive battle in which the child of God contends for his faith and his inheritance. "The weapons of our warfare are not carnal, but mighty through God to the pulling down of strongholds." These spiritual weapons are graphically described by the apostle: "Wherefore take unto you the whole armor of God, that ye may be able to withstand in the evil day, and having done all to stand. Stand therefore, having your loins girt about with truth, and having on the breastplate of righteousness; and your feet shod with the preparation of the gospel of peace, and above all, taking the shield of faith, wherewith ye shall be able to quench all the fiery darts of the wicked. And take the helmet of salvation, and the sword of the Spirit, which is the Word of God; praying always with all prayer and supplication in the Spirit, and watching thereunto with all supplication for all saints." Why all this spiritual armor, this watching, praying, and continual vigilance, if there be no spiritual foes outside of human nature? If the devil is a myth, and his "wiles" only a figure of speech, why has the Church been taught through the ages to watch, and fight, and pray, as if pursued by invisible spiritual foes, intent upon the destruction of every one whose faith falters?

THE LAST CONFLICT.

The scene of the devil's last conflict, and his ultimate overthrow, is laid in this world. It is in the book of Revelation, highly figurative or symbolical in the terms employed in the description, yet in scope and meaning quite in harmony with all that has been said herein. The "war in heaven" appears to be the theme; but that "war" was soon transferred to earth, and here beneath the clouds, where sin has so long held sway, the battle rages till the end:

"And there was war in heaven: Michael and his angels fought against the dragon; and the dragon fought and his angels, and prevailed not; neither was their place found any more in heaven. And the great dragon was cast out, that old serpent called the devil, and Satan, which deceiveth the whole world; he was cast out into the earth, and his angels were cast out with him." (Rev. xii, 7–9.) However much of the figurative may be found in this language, the fact is plain that the "great dragon" is called the devil and Satan, and he deceiveth the whole world. His contest with the angels has been given up, as he is banished from their realm, that he may engage all his forces in warfare against the Church on earth. This is now his sphere. "He was cast out into the earth, and his angels were cast out with him."

In this same chapter we read further: "And I heard a loud voice saying in heaven, Now is come salvation, and strength, and the kingdom of our God, and the power of his Christ; for the accuser of our brethren is cast down, which accused them before God day and night. And they overcame him by the blood of the Lamb, and by the word of their testimony; and they loved not their lives unto the death. Therefore rejoice, ye heavens, and ye that dwell in them. Woe to the inhabiters of the earth and of the sea! for the devil is come down unto you, having great wrath, because he knoweth that he hath but a short time." Symbol or no symbol, there is truth in this passage. "Woe to the inhabiters of the earth!" Sad the day when there was cause for this "woe." "For the devil is come down unto you!" In the light of all that has gone before, further exposition is needless. This world is now the battle-field. Wherever the war began, it is to be fought out here. Here Satan has his seat; here he has obtained dominion, and here he reigns, "the prince of this world;" and here all the forces of his kingdom are gathered, "the rulers of the darkness of this world," making their final struggle for the mastery. The prize is the control of the human race. For this prize every energy of the kingdom of darkness is enlisted.

This battle has been going on ever since the beginning of human history. It was inaugurated in Eden when the devil whispered, "Thou shalt not surely die." In the opening assault he carried the citadel of righteousness, and enthroned himself as "the prince of this world." Here he has remained. Under his sway idolatry has risen and flourished; superstition has taken the place of piety; sensuality has dominated, and man's enmity has turned against his kind, making the dark places of the earth the habitations of cruelty. The earth is the charnel-house of the nations and of the ages; the seat of war for the universe; the one spot in creation where sin abounds, and death blasts the life of all that live. The devil and his angels are here walking the earth unseen, mingling with the affairs of men, inciting evil passions, instigating unholy ambitions, wars, robberies, oppressions, and all disorders; employing every agency and instrumentality that can be used for the purpose of filling the earth with wretchedness and woe. Christians of the former generation portrayed this relentless warfare none too strongly when they sang:

> "Angels our march oppose,
>   Who still in strength excel,
> Our secret, sworn, eternal foes,
>   Countless, invisible;
> From thrones of glory driven,
>   By flaming vengeance hurled,
> They throng the air and darken heaven,
>   And rule this lower world."

Accepting, as we must, this Scriptural representation of the kingdom of darkness in its relation to this world, we see the reason why the incarnation of the Son of God was here, and not in some other world. "For this purpose the Son of God was manifested, that he might destroy the works of the devil." He came to grapple the usurper in his stronghold, where his temporary triumph was the greatest. He came here, where Satan has his home and kingdom; where are all the hosts of sin; where, as "prince of this world," his reign of darkness has been so long continued. Here, too, is the human race, the object of the devil's sorest hate and of heaven's deepest solicitude. Right here in the battle-field of the universe, in the center of the conflict, in the very heart of the devil's kingdom, and bearing the nature over which the arch-enemy had achieved his greatest victory, came the Son of man to redeem the fallen race, to break the power of Satan, bruise his head, and ultimately to cast him out. This conflict, which began in Eden, culminated at Calvary. The *crisis* came when the Son of God was lifted up from the earth. That was the turning-point. Till then was "the hour and power of darkness." In that hour Satan bruised the heel of the seed of the woman, and the seed of the woman bruised his head. The victory was assured when, on the morning of the third day, the Son of man proclaimed,

"I am he that liveth, and was dead; and, behold, I am alive for evermore, Amen; and have the keys of hell and of death." That shout of victory echoed through all the worlds, and rings down through the ages. The *crisis* is past! The work of redemption is complete. "Now shall the prince of this world be cast out."

This act of redemption laid the foundation for the kingdom of God upon earth. It fulfilled promise and prophesy, and provided for the overthrow of Satan's kingdom; for the ultimate casting out of "the prince of this world," whose reign was a usurpation, and whose power was the curse of man.

The prince of this world hath nothing in Christ. There is nothing in common between these two. "What concord hath Christ with Belial?" Their kingdoms are antagonistic. As darkness recedes before the advancing light, so with the coming of the kingdom of Christ the reign of "the prince of this world" passes away. While the provision for this final conquest is complete, and the result assured, the actual casting out of Satan is gradual and progressive. The soul of man is the area of the spiritual empire. When Christ is enthroned within, the evil prince is cast out. As one after another accepts Christ and is born into the kingdom, the kingdom of darkness suffers loss.

This work of translation from one kingdom into another has been going on through the ages. It is an individual experience. It requires the concurrence of the human will. Coercion is impossible. Force has no place in the contest. Progress is therefore slow, and sometimes the outcome appears uncertain. Herein is revealed the sphere of faith. All power is given unto the Son, who is able to conquer, and whose triumph is assured. The work of conversion will go on—the work of rescue—till the kingdoms of this world are become the kingdoms of our Lord and of his Christ. "He shall not fail nor be discouraged till he have set judgment in the earth." "For he must reign till he hath put all enemies under his feet." What was done provisionally in Christ's death, must be accomplished in fact through the power of his Spirit. The works of the devil must be destroyed as the final moral achievement.

The gospel of Jesus Christ is the ordained instrumentality for this work, and the Holy Spirit is the efficient agent. The subjugation of evil is essentially a divine work, yet one which God carries forward mainly through human instrumentalities, giving to man, redeemed from thralldom to sin and Satan an honorable part in the battle and in the triumph. Every convert becomes a soldier in this war, enlisted under the banner of the cross, and to every victor there is a crown. While the achievement is not by might nor by human power, but by the Spirit of the Lord, yet the part assigned to human agency is worthy of the noblest efforts that Christian faith can inspire. It is man doing God's work in God's name and through his power. The result is the dethronement of Satan, the casting out of "the prince of this world" from his usurped dominion, the emancipation of the nations from his long and cruel sway, and the uplifting of humanity to its rightful plane of life. It means the restoration of God's own life to human souls, the recovery of their powers from spiritual bondage to the noblest freedom through regeneration.

It means the destruction of idolatry and superstition, the removal of tyranny and oppression from human governments, the banishment of deception and fraud from social and business relations, the purification of personal and domestic life, and the establishment of peace on earth and good-will towards men. In a word, it means the conquest of this world for Christ, and all the blessedness of his reign and kingdom, with the banishment of the devil and his angels into "outer darkness," to await their final doom—the doom awaiting all the enemies of God, impressively symbolized by the "lake of fire and brimstone" and the "second death."

NOTE.

As supplementary to the foregoing, the following discourses or chapters on kindred topics are supposed to be not inappropriate. Indeed they seem to the author to be exactly in place. The doctrine of eternal retribution has logical relation to the existence, power, and doom of the devil. It must be understood, however, that the treatment of the themes introduced is not designed to be complete. It is purposely partial and brief, yet it is believed that it touches essential points, and indicates a line of argument which will stand in the future, as it has stood in the past, against the fiercest attacks the opposition can make. After all, there is an "eternal sin" and an "eternal condemnation."

S. M. M.

II.

THE UNPARDONABLE SIN.

"Hath never forgiveness."—MARK III, 29.

IT becomes all who believe the Scriptures to be divine to study them, not only in their historical, doctrinal, and ethical teachings, which are easily understood, but also in their intricate parts, and in what some regard as their "hard sayings." It is not to be denied that in the discourses of our Lord, as well as in the writings of the apostles, there are some things "hard to be understood," which ignorant and superficial thinkers are liable to "wrest unto their own destruction."

Such are the passages in which mention is made of the sin which can not be forgiven. While there is, and will be, more or less of mystery in these words, and while we may not be able to get hold of their full significance, it must be that a careful study of them will bring us to such a comprehension of their import as will be useful, and possibly be the means of ministering grace to our hearts, and certainly prove of service in warning the wayward. They are the words of the Lord, spoken on an occasion of great solemnity, and no doubt with an earnestness becoming their weight and the far-reaching results of their deliverance. We approach them reverentially, and desire to grasp the truth they contain with unbiased minds, and to give it the exact place in the great scheme of Christian doctrines to which it is entitled.

The subject of blasphemy necessarily belongs to the severer aspects of the system of Christianity. In the nature of things it must have to do with the doctrines of retribution. In some way it relates to the subject of diabolical influence and power, so that its treatment is not out of place in connection with a discourse on the existence and power of the devils. The word itself indicates the character of the offense. But for theological speculations concerning it there would be little occasion for looking beyond a proper definition of the term for its meaning. It is a sin usually expressed in words, a sin of the tongue, and yet the words come forth out of the heart, and express the condition of the heart. Blasphemy is found in that dark list of evils which the Lord said proceed from the heart and defile the man.

To blaspheme is to speak against; it is to express opposition, ridicule, contempt. It indicates spite, hatred, or animosity, and this state of feeling induced or accompanied by irreverence, so that while the heart is malignant, it is also light and superficial. Gross profanity is in common usage called blasphemy, and this designation is not inappropriate. He who uses the name of God flippantly and irreverently, makes near approaches to the sin of blasphemy, if he does not come to the full measure of this dreadful offense of deriding things sacred and divine. In the two blasphemies mentioned in the Scriptures to be considered, there is no intimation of any difference in the nature of the sin, so far as the outward form or expression is concerned, and certainly no marks are given by which the essence of one can be distinguished from the other, except the simple fact that one is against the Son of man, and the other is against the Holy Ghost. In fact and in substance or nature, they are the same. Both are blasphemy; both are found in words spoken, revealing the state of the heart; and in both there is the enmity and derision that would treat the work of God as the work of the devil.

With this general statement we group together the passages forming the groundwork and substance of our study: "Wherefore I say unto you, All manner of sin and blasphemy shall be forgiven unto men; but the blasphemy against the Holy Ghost shall not be forgiven unto men. And whosoever speaketh a word against the Son of man, it shall be forgiven him; but whosoever speaketh against the Holy Ghost, it shall not be forgiven him, neither in this world, neither in the world to come." (Matt. xii, 31, 32.) "Verily I say unto you, All sins shall be forgiven unto the sons of men, and blasphemies wherewith soever they shall blaspheme; but he that shall blaspheme against the Holy Ghost hath never forgiveness, but is in danger of eternal damnation." (Mark iii, 28, 29.) In Luke we have the same thought, but seemingly in another connection: "And whosoever shall speak a word against the Son of man, it shall be forgiven him; but unto him that blasphemeth against the Holy Ghost, it shall not be forgiven." (Luke xii, 10.)

It would be presumptuous to proceed in the study of these Scriptures, and of this great theme, without considering what has been said by others, and said so clearly and with such plausibility as to command very general acceptance, becoming an accredited part of the literature of the Church. In whatever way and to whatever extent we depart from the most prevalent interpretation, we want it understood that our position is taken deliberately, after weighing the subject in all its bearings, and under the best light at our command.

The first question that interests the student is as to the possibility of committing this greatest blasphemy, this unpardonable offense, at the present time, under the dispensation of the gospel. The motive that inclines the minister of Christ to answer this question in the negative, if he can find ground on which to base such an answer, is commendable in the highest degree. He is beset by anxious persons laboring under temptation, perplexed with doubts and fears, and buffeted by Satan to the border of despair, because of the apprehension that they have become guilty of this sin, and crossed the line of possible recovery to salvation. The minister feels how important it is to break this delusion of the devil, and to arouse hope in these anxious souls, so that he may lead them out of this darkness into the clear sunshine of the divine promises. In his anxiety at this point he reads again the interpretation that restricts the possibility of this sin to those who witnessed the miracles of Christ, and obstinately attributed them to the devil, and he feels constrained to accept the interpretation, and to use it for the relief of those who are in distress. His own feelings, as well as his interest in those whom he would lift out of despondency, incline him to wish this interpretation might be the correct one, and with the wish it becomes easy to persuade himself that it is even so. There is no doubt that this is the exact process through which many have reached the conclusion that the unpardonable sin belonged to the days of Christ, and can not be committed in our day.

Of course an opinion which has been so widely accepted must have something more than a wish behind it. There must be something in the wording of the Scriptures that looks in that direction, and gives apparent reasonableness to the construction. That such is the fact is readily conceded. Without the recognition of this condition of things our study of the subject would be incomplete. We must therefore look at the things which seem to countenance this interpretation, and see them as they are, and allow them all the weight that belongs to them. The assumption is that the offense consisted in attributing the miracles wrought by the Son of man to the devil. In doing this, these obstinate Jews rejected the evidence of their senses, closed their eyes to the clearest light that could fall upon them, trifled with Divine testimony, and evinced the deepest hatred to their Benefactor. Their sin was great. There is no doubt that it was blasphemy. The question is not as to whether they were guilty of blasphemy in their contemptuous treatment of Christ and his works, but whether they, and they alone, in this malignant hate, were guilty of blaspheming against the Holy Ghost. We must look at the whole record.

The connection shows that the Pharisees did what is alleged; they attributed his works to Satanic influence. They said: "This fellow doth not cast out devils, but by Beelzebub the prince of the devils." In reply to this accusation Jesus said: "Every kingdom divided against itself is brought to desolation: and every city or house divided against itself shall not stand: and if Satan cast out Satan, he is divided against himself; how shall then his kingdom stand? And if I by Beelzebub cast out devils, by whom do your children cast them out? Therefore they shall be your judges. But if I cast out devils by the Spirit of God, then the kingdom of God is come unto you." This accusation and interview was the occasion of these remarkable utterances on the subject of blasphemy; there is no doubt about that. Mark asserts that he spoke these things "because they said, He hath an unclean spirit." No worse accusation was ever brought against him; nothing could have been more offensive. Yet he bore it without resentment. While he spoke plainly of results, and warned his hearers of the dreadfulness of their sin, he avoided all appearance of personal pique or disposition to retaliate. But he recognized their blasphemy, and dealt faithfully with it. He knew that they spoke against him. They treated him with derision and contempt. In this they were guilty of blasphemy; but their blasphemy was against himself. It was the lesser grade of blasphemy, so to speak; the blasphemy that might be forgiven. This fact is clear, and it ought to be unquestionable, for it is vital to the right interpretation.

It is strange that this fact is so generally overlooked, while it is assumed that the more heinous blasphemy was committed in the presence of him who uttered these words. The Jews who rejected him, spoke against him and blasphemed, having him alone in mind while they burned with hatred towards him, thinking of no other. At best, they had vague conceptions of the Holy Ghost. He was not in their thoughts. His dispensation was not yet come. In the higher sense to which Jesus was training his disciples to look for his manifestation, "the Holy Ghost was not yet given, because that Jesus was not yet glorified." Blasphemy against him could hardly be expected before his fuller revelation, to take place after the departure of the Son of man. Why, then, this admonition? Why such a fearful denunciation of this greater sin, which had not yet been committed, and which was as yet scarcely possible? The language is *premonitory*. This is the key to the mystery. The Pharisees were speaking against the Son of man, were blaspheming him, charging him with being in collusion with the devil, and the spirit that prompted them to this would lead them to the still greater sin, the blasphemy against the Holy Ghost. So he warned them beforehand. His address to them was as if he had said: "I see the enmity of your hearts. You are enraged against me; you speak against me with all bitterness and venom; you despise me, and treat me as an impostor, and accuse me with having a devil. You see my works, and can not deny that devils are cast out; but you attribute what I do to Beelzebub, the prince of the devils. This is blasphemy. It is blasphemy against me—against the Son of man. It is a dreadful sin. It reveals a blinded, stubborn, malignant heart. But, mind you! wicked as is this blasphemy against me, it is less dangerous than what may follow. It may be forgiven. Repentance is possible. But I forewarn you! There is another blasphemy. I shall return to the Father, and the Holy Ghost will come; and when he is come, he may be spoken against. This spirit which you exhibit towards me will lead you to blaspheme against him. Whosoever shall speak against him, and blaspheme, shall not be forgiven. Be ye warned in time! He that shall treat the Holy Ghost as you have treated me, hath never forgiveness, but shall be in danger of eternal damnation."

This interpretation must strike every one as reasonable; and it is certainly more in harmony with the whole situation than is that which makes the witnesses of Christ's miracles guilty of the greater sin in charging him with having a devil. That view, so common and widespread, takes too little account of the first blasphemy—that against the Son of man; and it comes too nearly confounding the two blasphemies, leaving scarcely any room for distinguishing between them. Our Lord looked ahead. The premonitory character of his address must not be disregarded. He laid down an unchanging principle that pertained especially to the period of the development of the kingdom of God on earth, the time of the gospel, which is the dispensation of the Spirit. It is therefore proper to believe that resistance to the Holy Ghost under the gospel, when the Spirit of God does his most effective work, when carried to the point of utter rejection and malignant ridicule, will result in such a withdrawal of his presence, such an abandonment of the sinner to his obduracy, as to render him incapable of repentance, thereby making forgiveness impossible. The outward form of this sin is not described. Its nature is more important, and that is easily identified. It is resistance to the Spirit of God, carried to the extent of willful hatred and determined rejection. The heart of the impenitent can only reach the condition necessary to the final decision after repeated efforts, and after habitual resistance to the Divine warnings and strivings. But as certainly as it is a fact that sin blinds the heart and deadens the sensibilities, so certainly incorrigibility is possible, and reprobacy of mind becomes inevitable, placing the abandoned one outside the sphere of saving agencies.

If it be said that this interpretation, which recognizes this terrible sin as possible under the gospel, leaves the way open for temptation to despondency, to which so many are inclined when they become anxious about their souls, the answer is, that there is a better way of dealing with such than deceiving them with unsound expositions of the Word of the Lord. We must not handle the Word of God deceitfully; but by manifestation of the truth, commend ourselves to every man's conscience in the sight of God. The fact that they are anxious is proof positive that they are not abandoned of the Spirit. This should be urged upon their attention, and the evidences of his presence should be so described as to overcome their fears in this respect; and the Spirit of grace, working in them, will melt and win them to penitence.

The writings of the apostles contain many recognitions of the possibility and danger of incurring that degree of spiritual blindness and obduracy in which repentance is impossible. It is always held forth as the result of willfulness in resisting the light of truth, through the love of evil indulgence: "If our gospel be hid, it is hid to them that are lost, in whom the god of this world hath blinded the minds of them which believe not, lest the light of the glorious gospel of Christ, who is the image of God, should shine unto them." Paul again recognizes this condition in these strong words: "This I say, therefore, and testify in the Lord, that ye henceforth walk not as other Gentiles walk, in the vanity of their minds, having the understanding darkened, being alienated from the life of God through the ignorance that is in them, because of the blindness of their heart; who, being past feeling, have given themselves over unto lasciviousness, to work all uncleanness with greediness." Such language can not be understood except as descriptive of a moral degeneracy which excludes the capacity for repentance, and denotes the absence of gracious influences to the extent of abandonment to reprobacy and incorrigibility. That this state is sad beyond description is true, and that its possibility awakens in us emotions of anxiety is not to be disputed; yet the fact that it so impresses us does not authorize any attempt to ignore it, or to soften the import of the Divine teaching with regard to it. The dreadfulness of sin can not be too darkly pictured. God hates sin, and he intends that its desolating blight upon the human soul shall be so portrayed that men shall be fully warned, if they will only hear the truth.

It is a fact, not to be disregarded, that in the blinding and hardening process attributable to sin, Satan is always recognized as an active agent. He is the "god of this world" that blinds the minds of them that believe not. It is he that catcheth away the word sown in the heart. He is "the prince of the power of the air, the spirit that worketh in the children of disobedience." He who comes in his likeness, doing his work, deceiving and ensnaring men to their ruin, comes "after the working of Satan, with all power and signs and lying wonders, and all deceivableness of unrighteousness in them that perish, because they received not the love of the truth that they might be saved. For this cause God shall send them strong delusion, that they should believe a lie: that they all might be damned who believed not the truth, but had pleasure in unrighteousness." The moral disposition causing this abandonment of God, leaving men to the delusion and condemnation of the devil, is found in their unwillingness to "believe the truth," and in their taking "pleasure in unrighteousness." God's unchanging law of righteousness dooms all such to this condemnation. When the sinner stubbornly rejects the truth, and takes pleasure in unrighteousness, the Spirit of God leaves him to his own way, and he is "led captive by the devil at his will." This is not an arbitrary act, nor a spiteful resentment, the outgrowth of malignant passion, but the inevitable result of resistance to the supreme law of holiness, justice, and love. It may not be possible to identify the act which drives away the Holy Ghost, as perchance it may be the result of repeated and various acts of disobedience, a climax of rebelliousness; but the outcome is incapacity for return to repentance, and therefore the impossibility of forgiveness. The sin is unpardonable because of the deadness of the sensibilities. The soul that is "past feeling" is abandoned of God.

BEARING ON ETERNAL PUNISHMENT.

From this view we turn to study the result of this abandonment and the bearing of these Scriptures on the doctrine of eternal retribution. Negatively, it is clear enough that if the sinner can not be pardoned, he can not be saved.

Here we might stand, feeling perfectly sure that the possibility of the eternal punishment of the incorrigible is here taught with irresistible force and clearness; but justice is not done to the cause, and can not be, till we consider what is alleged on the other side, giving full credit to all efforts to interpret these passages in harmony with the doctrine which denies the ultimate loss of any soul. Something has been done in that direction, displaying critical skill, and great industry, and persistent purpose. Indeed, the latter is so conspicuous that its manifestation detracts from the force of the criticisms employed and relied upon in its defense.

It is needless to assume that those who deny eternal punishment are apt to adopt the definition of blasphemy against the Holy Ghost, which makes it an impossibility under the gospel dispensation. But they are bound to go beyond that, and get hold of a principle which excludes the possibility of its having ever been possible to any human being, in any age of the world, or else show that, having been committed, it is still possible to secure its cancellation and recovery from its power. This is a serious undertaking, but not a few have grappled with the problem with all the earnestness that determined resolution could inspire. Let us patiently study their efforts.

In the first place, they call our attention to the word "world," in the phrases, "Neither in this world, neither in the world to come." We are reminded that this word "world" is not *kosmos*, and does not mean the globe on which we live. This is a fact which we have no occasion to dispute. The word is not *kosmos*, but *aiōn*. It expresses duration, and not the material creation. In the next place, we are reminded that a large number of orthodox as well as other expositors render this word "age," and not "world." Here again we agree. There is not the slightest reason for disputing this fact. The next step is to quote some orthodox commentator, such as Dr. Adam Clarke, showing that the passage might be rendered, without violence, "Neither in this *age*, neither in the *age* to come." Many orthodox writers agree to this, and we make no contention against it; but still the issue is not reached, and much less is the decision of the issue in sight. We must follow our friends yet another step. It is then assumed that the phrase "this age," means the Jewish age; and that the phrase "the age to come," means the Christian age, or the gospel dispensation. This could also be admitted without serious result to the issue; but fidelity to exact truth will not justify the admission, and therefore we do not make it. But for the purpose of the present argument we proceed as if the point were conceded. Let us look into it, and see the outcome.

Here is a sin—a blasphemy—which may be forgiven; and here is another sin—another blasphemy—which may not be forgiven. The contrast is clear and sharp. The contention of our friends is that both may be forgiven. The burden of proof is upon them. Their duty in the premises is clear; and we credit them with the courage necessary to the task. Their rendering is this: "But whosoever speaketh against the Holy Ghost, it shall not be forgiven him, neither in this Jewish age, neither in the gospel age yet to come." It is possible that this looks less formidable, and perhaps a little milder than the common reading; but the question is, Does it show any progress toward the proof that this sin may be pardoned sometime? Of course it obscures the matter a little; but that is all. A sin committed under the Jewish age that could not be pardoned under that dispensation, nor yet under the gospel, does not have much prospect of forgiveness at any time. And, then, that other sweeping negative, which has no dependence on the word *age*, stands squarely across the path of all the criticisms and obscurations possible to our liberalistic friends: "But the blasphemy against the Holy Ghost shall not be forgiven unto men."

It has the appearance of boldness, not to say temerity, to look this declaration squarely in the face, and then affirm a doctrine which can not be true, unless there be some way to evade the force of its natural meaning. Pushed to this extremity, our liberalistic friends tell us that there is no special provision made for the forgiveness of this sin either in the Mosaic economy or in the gospel. Of course we admit this; but do not accept the statement as exhaustive of the meaning of the words, nor do we see wherein it relieves the system, whose life depends upon the denial of the possibility of any unpardonable sin. If the sin ever was committed by mortal man, it must be forgiven some time, or some one will be shut out of heaven forever.

It was not uncommon years ago for our Universalist friends, in view of the emergency this case brings them into, to advance the thought that the final escape from the consequence of this sin is in the resurrection of the dead, and therefore not in the Jewish or Christian age. But the idea of salvation from any sin in the resurrection is not insisted on now as formerly, for the reason that teachers of this school have changed their views of the resurrection itself, removing from themselves the ground on which they formerly builded their expectation of moral changes through resurrection power. They are compelled to recognize the fact that whatever their notion of the subjects, time, nature, or manner of the resurrection, it must belong to the gospel period, as it is indeed the crowning act of the redeeming scheme—the consummation of the kingdom of God. It therefore follows that forgiveness in the resurrection, if that might be affirmed, would still be forgiveness in the world or "age to come," if not in this age. To such straits are our friends driven, and yet without the slightest relief.

A desperate case necessitates desperate resorts. So, in their extremity, liberalists have given ample proof of their fertility in invention. Some have assumed that this whole matter of blasphemy against the Holy Ghost is a national affair; that the Jews as a nation rejected Christ, attributed his miracles to the devil, and incurred the guilt of a sin which could not be forgiven, but must be punished to the extent of its deserts; and that it was thus punished in the calamities that befell that people in the overthrow of their metropolis, the subversion of their polity, the desolation of their land, and their dispersion among the nations of the earth. The national sin and punishment of the Jews is a stupendous fact, attesting in the presence of nations and generations the truth of the predictions of Christ in the Holy Gospels; but the assumption that this blasphemy was a national sin is not only gratuitous, but preposterous, and inconsistent with the scope and language of the passages in question. A crime like rebellion, or the general prevalence of idolatry or unbelief or sensuality, might become, as it often does, a national sin; but here is plainly an individual sin, while the whole tenor of the words points to personal action and responsibility. It is "whosoever." There is nothing in all the connection to indicate any other than personal conduct. The sin is "blasphemy," speaking words against the Son of man and against the Holy Ghost. It is safe to say that the idea of a national offense and national punishment would never have been thought of in connection with these Scriptures, but for the predetermination to avoid their testimony to the fact of eternal punishment—a predetermination induced by the control which a favorite notion often obtains over the judgment and reason.

Thus every effort to interpret these words of our Lord, without involving the doctrine in question, becomes a mere subterfuge, having no support in criticism or sound exegesis. It is amazing that intelligent people are misled by such sophistries as appear in the endeavor to escape the truth to which we are shut up in these terrible words. Then, beyond the force of the unmistakable declaration, "It shall not be forgiven him, neither in this world, neither in the world to come," there is that other still stronger universal negative given in the record by Mark: "But he that shall blaspheme against the Holy Ghost hath never forgiveness." There is no way to evade this language. In it there is nothing equivocal, nothing ambiguous, nothing obscure. It stands as an impregnable wall across the path of every one who attempts escape. Its assertion must be admitted or denied; for it can neither be misunderstood nor distorted. "Hath never forgiveness" covers all worlds, all "ages," all dispensations and kingdoms, and all possible duration. "Hath never forgiveness!" These are the words of Jesus Christ—words of warning and pity welling from a heart of tenderness, the everlasting refutation of all doctrines that promise forgiveness to the impenitent, or salvation to the incorrigible.

III.

THE DURATION OF PUNISHMENT.

"Is in danger of eternal damnation."—MARK III. 29.
"Is guilty of an eternal sin."—REVISED VERSION.

WE follow the study of the unpardonable sin with a brief glance at the Scriptural authority for the doctrine of eternal punishment. Without any purpose to make the argument general or exhaustive, or to cover other ground than that indicated by the Scriptures already before us, we desire to weigh the terms expressive of duration, and candidly examine their import.

Since these Scriptures declare with certain voice that there is "an eternal sin," and that because it is unforgivable it is necessarily eternal, and its condemnation eternal; and since in our day many have been induced, by one pretext or another, to become doubtful or confused with regard to this doctrine; and since there is in the Churches an unaccountable trend towards loosening the lines of rigid teaching on this subject,— it seems well, and necessary indeed, for some one to recall attention, if possible, to the language of the Divine Teacher, and to the actual significance of his words touching the final condition of those who reject him. We do this, we trust, in the spirit that moved him to utter these strong words, remembering that the voice of warning is the most appropriate expression of love where danger threatens.

Of late years the literature of the Churches contains but little on this subject, leaving those who are just receiving their education in such matters very largely to the influence of the bold and unchallenged statements of those whose teachings are unsound and misleading. It is painful to realize the lack of information existing among young Christians on these weighty questions which divide between the evangelical and the liberalistic Churches of this country. A half, or even a third of a century ago, things were different in this regard. More attention was given to doctrines, and especially to the great doctrines which underlie the denominations, and distinguish them one from another. A prejudice against doctrines, or against their inculcation, has grown up, which bodes no good to the cause of truth; and particularly is this true with regard to those sterner teachings of our faith which portray the evils of sin, the power of the devil, the depravity of man, and the destiny of the wicked. The result is, that the average congregation, in our cities especially, can be filled with heresy from the pulpit without suspecting it, if only the discourse be clothed in attractive garb and take on an ethical pretentiousness. The exigency demands that the doctrine of eternal retribution be again set forth as it appears in the Holy Scriptures.

In these Scriptures relating to the sin of blasphemy, the assertion is that the incorrigible shall be "in danger of eternal damnation." The language is plain and vigorous, and emphasized by the fact that it describes the result of sin which "hath never forgiveness." As honest students of the Word, we are bound to face the strongest language without bias, and to seek its proper meaning with an unswerving purpose to accept it as authoritative, regardless of any personal preferences we may possess. These two phrases belong together, and should be studied together: "Hath never forgiveness," "Shall be in danger of eternal damnation." We grant that this old English word "damnation," is simply the equivalent of condemnation; but the meaning is not changed. "Eternal condemnation" may have a milder sound to some ears, and may be preferred on that account, without any softening of the dreadful reality expressed. Whosoever has committed the sin which "hath never forgiveness," is necessarily doomed to "eternal condemnation."

Just here we are reminded that in the New Version this word "condemnation" does not appear. The revisers recognizing another Greek text, in place of the phrase, "Shall be in danger of eternal damnation," give us as the better rendering, "Shall be guilty of an eternal sin." Accepting this rendering, its bearing on the doctrine in question becomes a matter of interest. To be "guilty of an eternal sin" is a serious something. It is a guilt which abides, which is never removed, which "hath never forgiveness." No mitigation is found in this reading. The doctrine is not modified in the least degree. Our ears are not yet familiar with the sound of these words; but there must be such a thing as an "eternal sin." Not that the act is forever in process without being completed; nor yet that the sin is being forever repeated, making an infinite series of transgressions; but the sin once committed is a fact for eternity, and the guilt once upon the soul remains uncanceled, unforgiven, unexpiated. The condemnation of this sin is an "eternal condemnation."

THE TWO GREEK WORDS.

This brings us to the study of the words rendered "eternal." Around these words has gathered the smoke of battle for generations. Here the enemies of the doctrine of eternal punishment have massed their forces; here they have displayed their longest lines and their heaviest arms, and in the presence of this strong orthodox citadel, which has never been captured, they have assumed the airs of victors, and persuaded themselves that they were in possession, when they have neither passed a trench, nor taken a redoubt. As an invincible stronghold, unmoved in her quiet security, this old fortress sends forth an occasional shot from her ramparts into the camp of her enemies to assure them that she is still impregnable.

It is needless to retrace the literature of this old controversy, and yet the most that can now be said has been said before. Our aim shall, therefore, be at clearness and directness, rather than at novelty or originality.

The two Greek words, *aiōn* and *aiōnios*, are the words in dispute. The latter is a derivative of the former, and, so far as duration is concerned, both express exactly the same thing. They are, therefore, to be treated as different forms of the same word. All concede that they express duration; but the dispute is as to whether they express limited or unlimited duration. Our contention is that they express unlimited duration, and that they are the best words in the Greek language to express an endless condition, whether that condition be good or bad. Because of the great amount of effort that has been made to disprove this position, more of detail in analysis and illustration will be allowable than would be necessary under other circumstances.

Much has been said about the primary and secondary meaning of these words. What we want to get at is their proper meaning as used in the New Testament, and especially as they occur in connection with punishment. That they are used in connection with the punishment of the wicked, is a fact not to be disputed; but the question is as to their meaning when so used, and as to whether they are to be taken in their primary and literal signification, or in a secondary or figurative sense. The particular phases of the issue will appear as we proceed.

The word *aiōn* is composed of two words, *aei*, ever; and *ōn*, being; literally, ever being. In order to see its force, as a word expressive of duration, we will glance briefly at the use of *aei*, when it occurs alone or uncompounded. A few instances will suffice. "And the multitude crying aloud, began to desire him to do as he had ever—*aei*—done unto them." (Mark xv, 8.) "Ye stiffnecked and uncircumcised in heart and ears, ye do always—*aei*—resist the Holy Ghost." (Acts vii, 51.) "For we which live are always—*aei*—delivered unto death." (2 Cor. iv, 11.) "Wherefore I was grieved with this generation, and said they do always—*aei*—err in their heart." (Heb. iii, 10.) "The Cretians are always—*aei*—liars." (Titus I, 12.) "But sanctify the Lord God in your hearts, and be ready always—*aei*—to give an answer to every man that asketh you a reason of the hope that is in you." (1 Peter iii, 15.) "Wherefore I will not be negligent to put you *always* in remembrance of these things." (2 Peter I, 12.) In all these places, and in many more, this word *aei* is used in the sense of always or continually, expressing uninterruptedness of existence or of habit. The lexicons define it "always, ever, aye; uninterruptedly, continually, perpetually." Donegan applies it to the circumstance of magistrates succeeding one another in uninterrupted succession. The conclusion is, therefore, irresistible, that when joined with the word *ōn*, or being, it denotes uninterrupted, and therefore ceaseless, duration. This is its first and most literal meaning, the sense it always conveys, except when used in an accommodated way, as when applied to things which are by their nature limited as to duration. Even then the limiting circumstance is not in the word, but in the nature of the thing to which it is applied. It expresses the entire duration of "the everlasting hills."

It is conceded on all sides that this word is often used to convey the idea of endless duration, and used for that purpose when the scope of the thought would demand the employment of the strongest and most unequivocal word in the language to express the thought.

This is certainly true when the design is to express the duration of the being and perfections of God, the throne and dominion of Jesus Christ, and the happiness of the saints in heaven. If the language contained a word that would more strongly or more certainly convey the idea of endless duration than this word does, it would have been used when these glorious things of eternity were described as to their duration; but this word, and no other, was used for this purpose, and used continually in such relations. This tremendous fact ought to be decisive as to the meaning of the word, and it is decisive, whether those having a doctrine to maintain which will not bear the admission, agree to it or not. Nor can it be that the word is used in an accommodated or secondary sense for this high purpose. If there is a truth in the universe worthy of declaration definitely, unequivocally, and in language incapable of being misunderstood, it is the truth which relates to the eternity of God, and the endlessness of heaven. It can not be that such truth is revealed only in words used in an accommodated, metaphorical, or secondary sense.

It is not disputed that words are sometimes used in a secondary or accommodated sense; but this fact does not authorize arbitrary juggling. The accommodated use of words must have some law and some limitation. Words which properly express unlimited duration may be accommodated to the expression of limited time, where the limit is apparent, or where the limiting circumstance is known; but it is not possible to make a word expressive of definite or limited time, express more than it contains in its literal or proper signification. A year can not be used to mean a century; nor can the word century be extended to mean a millennium. The greater contains the less, but the less does not contain the greater. A part does not contain the whole. Time does not contain eternity. So a word for limited time can not express unlimited duration. When a word whose proper meaning is endless duration is applied to things of earth or things that perish, it is necessarily used in an accommodated sense, the limiting circumstance being in the nature of the thing that can not endure forever. It is plain, therefore, that the word which expresses the endless duration of God and his throne, must contain the idea of endless duration as its primary and literal meaning. This is our contention; but those who deny the eternity of punishment, contend that the word in question means only limited time, properly, and that it is used to express the eternity of God's throne and kingdom in a secondary or accommodated sense. They hold that it expresses more than it contains; that its meaning is expanded; that in some mysterious way this word leaps beyond itself to express the endlessness of the kingdom of glory, while it shrivels into imperative limitations when applied to the condemnation of sin, which " hath never forgiveness."

Finding, then, as we do, both from its composition and its use, that this word literally means endless duration, and is properly rendered "everlasting" and "eternal," the question arises, and is easily answered, as to whether it must be taken in its primary, literal sense, when it is employed in connection with punishment to express its duration. The answer is, All words are to be understood in their literal or primary sense, unless there is something in their use to clearly indicate the contrary. This word, *aiōnion*, literally means "everlasting," and it is used to express the duration of punishment again and again, in the Scriptures, and always without any notice or intimation of a figurative, accommodated, or secondary use, and it is so used that there can be no limiting circumstance, unless it be found in the nature of the thing to which it is applied. It is applied to punishment, and unless there is something in the nature of punishment that limits its duration, it must mean endless punishment.

Will our friends of the opposition contend that there is somewhat in the nature of punishment that limits it to temporary duration? It is not sufficient to insist that the design of punishment implies its limitation; for the design of punishment is not now in the account. To bring it in at this point is to assume the point in dispute. It is to beg the question. We affirm nothing in this contention with regard to the nature or the design of punishment. The simple issue is as to its duration, its endlessness, its finality. The word "everlasting" expresses it. It is everlasting unless it is limited in its own nature. Then the limitation is not in the word, but in the nature of the punishment. There is nothing in the nature of punishment that can limit it as to duration, unless it be in the nature of the subject of the punishment; that is, in the sinner condemned to the punishment. If the immortality of the sinner should fail, and the moral ruin wrought within him destroy sensibility and consciousness, that might modify the punishment in its nature and result, but it would neither terminate the condemnatory sentence nor reverse it. The "condemnation" would still be "eternal." In this sense the punishment would be unending, and the word "everlasting" would express it literally and properly.

Whenever the word *aiōn* is construed with the preposition *eis*, especially in New Testament Greek, it invariably signifies endless duration. This statement is so certainly correct that there is not the slightest danger of contradiction; and yet it means much in this discussion. Not that the preposition adds to the duration expressed by the word itself, for that is impossible; but it marks its application, and denotes that it is to be taken in its full and proper sense. It is used in this way about sixty times in the New Testament. In fifty-four places it undeniably expresses endless duration. In the remaining six places its application is to punishment, and no sign appears that it is not used in its uniform signification. Now, if in fifty-four instances this word is used in this way in the sense of endless duration, is it not reasonable to assume that it bears the same import in the other six places, seeing there is no limiting word or circumstance to forbid it? The phrase *eis tous aiōnas tōn aiōniōn*, commonly rendered "for ever and ever," occurs eighteen times in the New Testament. In fifteen instances it expresses the continuance of the glory, perfection, government, and praise of God. The idea of endlessness is its burden in all these places. In one of the remaining instances it is applied to the righteous in the future world, who shall reign "for ever and ever." In the other two instances it is applied to punishment. Of a class of impenitent sinners it is said that "the smoke of their torment ascendeth up for ever and ever." In the remaining passage it is said of the devil, the beast, and the false prophet, that "they shall be tormented day and night for ever and ever." Conceding that there is figurative language in these Scriptures, and that the symbolism of this book is not easily understood, the fact still stands that the phraseology is that which expresses endlessness. Whatever the import of the symbols, the words bear their proper meaning, and *represent* a state of endless perdition. Then we ask again, Is it reasonable to suppose that the Spirit of God would inspire his servant to use this phrase sixteen times to denote a duration absolutely endless, and twice to denote something absolutely different, without the slightest indication of a different import?

The derivative, *aiōnios*, is used seventy-one times in the New Testament. Five times it expresses the duration of punishment. In all the other instances it unquestionably denotes endless duration. In some places the contrast is made between the final condition of the righteous and the wicked, and this word is so employed to express the duration of the condition of both classes, that if there were any difference in the duration, common honesty would demand that it be intimated, and without the intimation deception would certainly be the result. Then the question recurs, Is it not reasonable to conclude that the word bears the same meaning in the five instances in which it applies to punishment that it does in the sixty-six instances? If so, the endlessness of future punishment is taught in the Holy Scriptures beyond the shadow of a doubt. The words expressive of duration, applied again and again to the ultimate outcome of a life of sin, cover all possible existence in the everlasting state.

We sum up as follows: 1. The radical import of *aiōn* and of *aiōnion* is unlimited duration. 2. It is a correct rule that these words, as all words, should be understood in their proper, radical, or primary sense, except where there is some word or circumstance which clearly limits their meaning. 3. Words expressive of duration may be restricted in their application to less than their literal and primitive import, but they can not be enlarged so as to express more than they contain. 4. When the preposition *eis* stands with *aiōn*, that word is never used in a limited sense; and it is thus found in connection with future punishment. 5. There is nothing in the nature of punishment to restrict the meaning of the word, or to prevent it from having its proper sense, unless the subject of the punishment should drop out of being, in which event the judgment decree or sentence to eternal punishment would not be reversed. The irreversible doom of the sinner would be effectual, and the word expressive of unlimited duration would have appropriate use.

OTHER WORDS.

The position above summarized will be confirmed if it be seen to be impossible to find another word in the Greek that will so well express the idea of unlimited duration. In their stress of anxiety to make a point against the doctrine of eternal retribution, its opponents sometimes urge an inquiry like this: If God intended the doctrine of eternal punishment to be believed, why is it not set forth in unambiguous language—in the use of words which so clearly express the idea of endless duration that their meaning can not be misunderstood? This implies that the terms in which this doctrine is taught in the Scriptures, the words already considered, are ambiguous, which we deny, and have shown to be untrue; and it also implies that there were other words in the language that might have been employed, that were less ambiguous, and better calculated to express clearly and forcefully the idea of endless duration. So important has this been deemed that serious efforts have been made to establish the proposition. The words claimed as expressing endless duration better than those employed for that purpose have been specified, which, of course, is the only way of testing the matter, and we must therefore look at the words indicated, and weigh the claim set up for them.

The claim that other words express endless duration better than *aiōn* and *aiōnion* is a reflection on the wisdom of the sacred writers; for there is no doubt that, when they wrote of the duration of the kingdom and glory of God, they desired to express themselves clearly, and did the best they knew how to give expression and emphasis to the thought. But if they passed by words better adapted to their purpose, and chose words of ambiguous and uncertain import, they did it ignorantly, or carelessly, or with purpose to be obscure. Whatever view one takes of the matter, if the facts be as alleged, either the wisdom or the honesty of these writers is impeached.

It will appear on examination that the words specified by the opposition, in behalf of which this claim is made, do not express duration at all directly, but only imply it; so that, at best, their implication of duration is only a consequential idea, not contained in the words at all. They express the quality of substances, or the nature of things or offices, and have only an incidental relation to duration. Two of these words relate to the resurrection-body, and express its incorruptibility and immortality, thereby implying continued existence; but they do not mention or relate to duration. These are *aphtharsia*, incorruption; and *athanasia*, immortality. It is simply ridiculous to hold that these express endless duration at all, and much more so to insist that they do it better than the words chosen by the inspired writers for that purpose. In the same interest, *amarantos* is sometimes mentioned. It is of the same class as the two just considered. It expresses the quality of things, and not duration; meaning unfading, as where the inheritance is described by Peter as "incorruptible, undefiled, and that *fadeth not away.*" It was never designed to express duration, is not adapted to that end, and it is absurd to mention it in that connection.

There are yet two other words for which this claim is made, to which we must give a little more attention. The first is *akatalutos*, which is translated endless. It occurs in Hebrews vii, 16: "Who is made, not after the law of a carnal commandment, but after the power of an *endless* life." The life mentioned is that which pertained to our Lord's priesthood, and stands opposed to the individual tenure of office under the law of succession in the Aaronic priesthood, wherein men were not permitted to continue by reason of death. No high priest could remain throughout the dispensation. The word is compounded of *a*, negative, and *kataluoō*, to dissolve, and means, literally, indissoluble. *Kataluoō* is from *kata*, down, and *luō*, to loose, and is defined in the lexicons, "To unloose, loosen, dissolve; to demolish, destroy, overthrow; cancel, annul, abrogate; depose, desist from, lay down office." The priests, under the law, were compelled to lay down office, to dissolve connection with it, because of death; but when Christ entered upon his priestly duties, he possessed a life that was indissoluble, and therefore he continues in the priesthood throughout the dispensation. His life is endless, in fact; but the word here rendered endless relates to its permanency, and only consequentially to its duration. It is easily seen that duration is not its meaning. It is endless because it can not be dissolved; and the word expresses its indissolubility directly, and suggests duration secondarily. The indissolubility of Christ's tenure of the priestly office is the great thought. It would be exceedingly inappropriate to use this word where the simple idea of duration was to be expressed; and our Lord and his apostles are not chargeable with incompetency for not preferring it when they wished to express endless duration.

The next word to which our attention is called is found in Heb. x, 12: "But this man, after he had offered one sacrifice for sins, *forever* sat down on the right hand of God." The word here rendered forever is *diēnekes*, the neuter of *diēnekēs*, which is from *dia*, through, and *ēnekēs*, extensive; and is rendered "continuous, uninterrupted, constant, perpetual; lasting, durable, extended; a state of uninterrupted protraction." It is therefore properly enough translated "forever" in the place where it is found, having reference to the fact that Christ so completely atoned for sin by his one sacrifice that his work will never have to be repeated. Although he continues in the office of high priest, making intercession for the Church, there will be no occasion for another sin-offering. "For by one offering he hath perfected—*diēnekes*—perpetually, or forever, them that are sanctified." The radical idea of this word is uninterruptedness. It applies to something uniform—steady, persistent, perpetual; so that it has an element of finality in it, and requires duration as an auxiliary, or secondary idea; but that it expresses duration as its radical import is far from the truth. It is not defined by lexicographers as is *aiōnion*—everlasting, eternal, endless;

nor is it recognized as containing the time-element, expressing duration as its proper meaning. Neither is it employed to express the duration of the perfections, kingdom, glory, or praise of God; nor the endless life and blessedness of the righteous. If it were, in fact, better adapted to convey the idea of endless duration than *aiōn* or *aiōnion*, it is scarcely conceivable that it would have been omitted when the sacred writers wanted to express that idea in the clearest possible way.

We have a right to be amazed at the temerity of our friends of the opposition. They hold that the fact that this word is not used in the Scriptures to express the duration of punishment is an argument against the eternity or finality of punishment; but they do not see any argument against the eternity of the happiness of the saints in heaven in the fact that it is never used to express the duration of that happiness. The truth is, not one of these words is the proper word for endless duration; and that accounts for the fact that neither of them is used to express the eternity of the happiness of the saved, the punishment of the wicked, nor the perfections of the Deity. It is the madness of folly to try to fix upon either of these words—Scripture words as they are—the meaning that Scriptural usage and all the authorities fix upon *aiōn* and *aiōnios*. This is what the opposers of the doctrine of eternal punishment are doing, under the pressure, no doubt, of an emergency which is keenly felt; and their effort to deprive the words which do express endless duration, of their proper significance, is a failure sufficiently conspicuous to reveal the folly of the undertaking.

We turn away from this discussion, which is but fairly opened, because of limitations imposed upon this writing which we must observe. The subject is great, worthy of thorough treatment, and the material is abundant. The application of the principles above set forth to the Scriptures, in which the terms occur, would be an interesting exercise, and would in every instance confirm the positions taken, and bring the doctrine maintained into the light of Scriptural demonstration; but we leave that to the reader, believing that every one capable of comprehending the argument, can use these principles in the solution of all the problems arising from the particular passages bearing on the subject. The ethical aspects of the doctrine have not been brought in for lack of space, and for the reason that our sole purpose was to present the foundation in the terms which the Scriptures use, and to guard against the glosses of the opposition. It will be observed, also, that we have strenuously avoided considering all questions relating to the nature or results of future punishment. There is a constant tendency in the minds of most people to drift from the simple point of the proof of duration to the place, agencies, nature, and effects of the eternal retribution so surely taught in the Scriptures. Most of these incidental studies must be largely conjectural, since revelation does not deal with them, and the diversion of the mind to their consideration obscures the main issue, and distracts thought when it needs concentration.

There is, of course, a very natural interest felt in all these matters; and, after the foundation is firmly established in the irrefragable proofs of the fact and duration of future punishment, it is well to gather all the light available with reference to the Divine methods and purpose in punishment, the provision made for it, and the outcome in the effect it may have on individuals and on the moral universe. Some questions will arise in such an investigation that must both puzzle and perplex our reason, because the factors necessary to the satisfactory answer are not furnished in the Scriptures, and can not be found in any philosophy within our reach. In such conditions wisdom dictates the recognition of the limitations of the finite understanding, and suggests that duty requires contentment with "those things which are revealed," so long as in our pupilage "we know in part," and "see through a glass darkly." If an understanding of the nature and results of eternal punishment had been necessary to our warning or edification, these things would probably have been made as clear to us as is the fact itself. With us the great thing is the fact. The final decree of judgment consigns the devil and his angels, and all the ungodly of our race, to a perdition out of which there is no redemption. This is their "everlasting punishment." Whether in the oncoming ages their sensibilities remain keenly alive, or deaden into unconsciousness, their doom is alike irreversible. Beyond the realm of light and grace their abode is "outer darkness." Where the Judge Eternal places them, we must leave them.

The End.

www.ingramcontent.com/pod-product-compliance
Lightning Source LLC
Chambersburg PA
CBHW020241170426
43202CB00008B/170